COOKIN CRUNK

BIANCA PHILLIPS

EATIN' VEGAN IN THE DIRTY SOUTH

Book Publishing Company

Summertown, Tennessee

Library of Congress Cataloging-in-Publication Data

Phillips, Bianca.
   Cookin' crunk : eatin' vegan in the Dirty South / by Bianca Phillips.
     p. cm.
   Includes index.
   ISBN 978-1-57067-268-2 (pbk.) — ISBN 978-1-57067-925-4 (e-book)
  1. Vegan cooking.   2. Cooking, American—Southern style.   I. Title.
   TX837.P523 2012
   641.5'636—dc23

                                      2012011944

Cover and interior design: John Wincek
Cover and insert photos: Andrew William Schmidt
Food styling: Barbara Jefferson, Ron Maxen

Printed on recycled paper

Book Publishing Co. is a member of Green Press Initiative. We chose to print this title on paper with postconsumer recycled content, processed without chlorine, which saved the following natural resources:

41 trees
1,202 pounds of solid waste
18,995 gallons of wastewater
4,203 pounds of greenhouse gases
17 million BTUs of total energy

For more information, visit greenpressinitiative.org.

Paper calculations from Environmental Defense Paper Calculator, edf.org/papercalculator.

Printed in the United States

Book Publishing Company
P.O. Box 99
Summertown, TN 38483
888-260-8458
bookpubco.com

ISBN 13: 978-1-57067-268-2

18 17 16 15 14 13   2 3 4 5 6 7 8 9

Calculations for the nutritional analyses in this book are based on the average number of servings listed with the recipes and the average amount of an ingredient if a range is called for. Calculations are rounded up to the nearest gram. If two options for an ingredient are listed, the first one is used. The analyses include oil used for frying. Not included are optional ingredients and serving suggestions.

Contents

When I launched Vegan Crunk, my vegan food blog, in late 2007, I wanted a name that conveyed both my passion for veganism and my Southern roots. "Crunk," a Southern slang term that means "to get excited" (and also describes a style of raw rap music from Memphis, Tennessee), immediately came to mind.

I must admit that I get pretty crunk about cooking simple recipes handed down by generations of great Southern cooks. Crunk is about passion. It's about having pride in where you come from. It's about creating no-frills, no-nonsense dishes that warm the soul and keep rich Southern traditions alive. That's exactly what I aim to do in this book.

I grew up in northeast Arkansas and transplanted myself about sixty miles south to Memphis only weeks after finishing college at Arkansas State University. I've never lived more than an hour from the banks of the muddy Mississippi River—the iconic waterway that defines the deep-down Dirty South.

For the record, the South isn't really all that dirty. It's certainly no dirtier than any other place in the world. But the phrase "Dirty South" doesn't have much to do with dirt in the physical form. It has more to do with keepin' it real. Southerners never stray far from tradition. We tend to do what our mamas did and what our grandmamas did before them.

To live in the Dirty South means drinking sweet tea on wraparound porches. It means getting lost in the beautiful song of cicadas on humid summer nights. It means crumblin' homemade cornbread into a lovingly prepared bowl of soup beans, or drippin' watermelon juice down your chin as you take the first bite of a ripe summer melon.

First on my Vegan Crunk blog and now in this book, I aim to keep the rich and passionate cooking culture of the Dirty South alive by removing the meat, eggs, and dairy products from classic family recipes that have been handed down for generations. Being vegan shouldn't preclude anyone from enjoying soul food. In fact, because the recipes in this book don't contain meat and other animal products, eating them will enrich your soul—and save animals' lives in the process.

Acknowledgments

This book wouldn't have been possible without the support, recipe contributions, and inspiration from two amazingly strong women—Delories Phillips (my mama) and Ruth Phillips (my granny).

I began following my mama around in the kitchen when I was just a little girl, and I owe my culinary inclination to her influence. I used to tease her when she read cookbooks at night the way most people read novels. Now I do the same thing. When I went vegetarian at age fourteen and vegan at age twenty-four, my mama patiently tweaked her family recipes to be free of meat, eggs, and dairy. There's no kinder or gentler soul in the world than my mama.

Then there's Granny (my daddy's mama). Through her delicious, soul-warming country cookin', she taught me to appreciate the rich food culture of my Southern roots. When Granny heard I was working on a Southern vegan cookbook, she quickly learned how to create delicious dairy-free, egg-free desserts and entrées from her repertoire of family recipes. Not only did she spend countless hours creating recipes for this book, she also suggested plenty of Southern dishes and meals for me to veganize.

Special gratitude is owed to David Phillips (my daddy) for being a relentless supporter of my cookbook project and the Vegan Crunk blog that inspired this book; to my me-maw (my mama's mama), who, despite her disdain for cooking, was an appreciative taste tester at many family meals; and to my pa (my daddy's father), who sampled most all of Granny's veganized creations (probably without even realizing the dishes were vegan).

Also, thanks to my partner, Paul Dillard, a relentless promoter, for pushing my blog and cookbook project to everyone who would listen; to my best friend, Sheridan Essman, who went vegetarian (and later vegan) after reading about animal suffering and subsequently tested numerous recipes on her friends and coworkers; to Stephanie Roy, the best vegan baker in the world, for testing recipes and offering baking advice when my experiments failed; and to my friend Wes, an old-school Southern cook, who introduced me to hominy and fried cucumbers.

Finally, I'd like to thank the talented testers and blogger friends whose advice was critical in perfecting the recipes contained in these pages: Alison, Breedale, Carol, Carrie, Chelsea, Colette, Courtney, Deborah, Happyface Jessy, Jennifer Molica, Jenn Lynskey, Karen Lucchesi, Laura from Peace By Pastries, Leslie Coleman, Lindsay Ingalls, Megan Duke, Miss V, Nora Kuby, Paula, Pink-Haired Cyn, Radioactive Vegan, River Bounds, Ryan, Trinity, VeggieLow, and Wetland Susie.

Introduction

For generations, meat and other animal products have characterized the cuisine of the American South. Besides serving up main courses of fried chicken, pulled pork barbecue, and crawfish, old-time Southern cooks often flavor their veggies with bacon fat and lard. Ugh.

But you won't find any ham hocks in these collard greens. There's no pork sausage in this gravy, and there's certainly not a hint of chicken in these dumplin's. *Cookin' Crunk: Eatin' Vegan in the Dirty South* offers more healthful vegan versions of traditional Southern fare.

From cheese-free Ro*Tel dip and country-fried tempeh steak to eggplant jambalaya and stewed okra and tomatoes, *Cookin' Crunk* offers plenty in the way of comfort food with a meat-free twist. Of course, there are also plenty of sweet treats free of eggs and dairy, like dark chocolate pecan pie, blackberry cobbler, and peanut butter and banana "Elvis" cupcakes.

Most of my recipes are fairly simple, although some require advance preparation. I'm not a trained chef, just a Southern gal who grew up hovering around the knees of my mama and granny in the kitchen. As a result, my recipes are far from pretentious and gourmet—just simple, comfort food free of meat and other animal products. Any recipes that do require a little extra work, such as making homemade seitan or barbecue sauce, can be simplified by using store-bought versions of the homemade ingredients. Some recipes suggest marinating tofu or tempeh for eight to twelve hours. I've made a note in these recipes and any others where more than one hour of advance preparation is required.

There are many vegan versions of conventional ingredients, such as mayonnaise and margarine. Though any brand may be used for the recipes in this book, I've mentioned some of my favorites in the section The Southern Vegan Pantry (page 1).

One thing you'll notice is that I don't shy away from frying foods. After all, side dishes like fried squash or fried green tomatoes are a deep-rooted Southern tradition. However, I do attempt to "healthify" some greasy Southern fare with baked alternatives. You'll find a good balance of fried and baked dishes in this book.

Many of the recipes in this book are veganized versions of my family's signature dishes, such as an egg-free version of Granny's coconut pie and a version of Mama's cornbread dressin' that uses vegetable broth instead of chicken stock. Removing the meat, eggs, and dairy products from these family classics keeps traditional Southern foodways alive, while also allowing vegans, vegetarians, and anyone who cares about healthful eating to enjoy the down-home fare handed down by so many generations of talented Southern cooks.

The Southern Vegan Pantry

There's nothing like a well-stocked pantry (and refrigerator) to encourage home cookin'. Who wants to run down to the grocery store before every meal? Here's a quick list of some of the most common ingredients in my veganized Southern dishes. Keep your kitchen stocked with these foods, and you'll be cookin' up down-home country meals in no time.

Adobo seasoning. A flavorful seasoning salt used in Spanish cooking, adobo seasoning is available in most supermarkets in the spice section or with the Latin American foods. It typically contains black pepper, cayenne or other chiles, cumin, garlic powder, and oregano, among other ingredients. If you can't find it, substitute an all-purpose seasoning salt.

Agave nectar. Since vegans avoid honey, the increased availability of agave nectar is a welcome development, as this thick liquid sweetener is an ideal substitute. Made from the agave plant (the same plant used to make tequila!), this shelf-stable sweetener has a lower glycemic index than white sugar, so it doesn't spike your blood sugar. It's available in raw, light, and dark varieties, and I use them all interchangeably. It dissolves quickly in liquids, making it an excellent sweetener for iced tea.

Applesauce, unsweetened. I substitute unsweetened applesauce for oil in a few of my dessert recipes. The result is moist baked goods with a lower fat content.

Black-eyed peas. Black-eyed peas are a staple in Southern cooking. I keep canned peas on hand, and I always rinse and drain them before using. One 14-ounce can of black-eyed peas equals about 1$\frac{1}{2}$ cups of cooked dried peas. Feel free to substitute frozen or dried black-eyed peas, cooking them according to the package directions and measuring out what you'll need for the recipe. (About 1$\frac{1}{4}$ cups of dried black-eyed peas will make about 1$\frac{1}{2}$ cups cooked.) Or use shelled fresh black-eyed peas, if you can find them, cooked in boiling water until tender.

Black salt. If you love being vegan but miss the taste of eggs, black salt is a must-try. This age-old Indian condiment (also known as *kala namak*) derives its spot-on eggy taste from trace amounts of sulfur compounds. The salt isn't actually black at all; it's pinkish in color. Black salt tends to lose some of its potent flavor when cooked, so I prefer to add it to cold salads and spreads. You can find black salt at any well-stocked Indian market or online.

Breadcrumbs. Keep both panko and dry whole wheat breadcrumbs on hand for the recipes in this book. Now popular and widely available, panko is a flaky type of breadcrumb originally used in Japanese cooking. It makes a lovely breading for fried and baked Southern foods. Whole wheat breadcrumbs are perfect for topping casseroles.

Brown rice. Brown rice is a more wholesome alternative to white rice because the bran is left intact. I never use white rice in my recipes, but feel free to substitute white rice if you wish. Brown rice takes longer to cook—about 45 minutes compared to only 20 minutes for white rice—so I recommend cooking brown rice ahead of time for use in most recipes.

Cajun seasoning. I call for Cajun seasoning in some of these recipes. It usually contains garlic powder and onion powder, along with such spices as black pepper, celery seed, chile peppers, and dry mustard, but the different brands can be quite distinctive. I'm partial to Tony Chachere's Creole Seasoning, but you should try various brands to find the ones you like best. If you don't have Cajun seasoning on hand, substitute an all-purpose seasoning salt.

Chickpea flour. Also available in Indian markets as *besan* flour, chickpea flour makes a great addition to homemade seitan, lending the wheat meat a more tender texture than when it's made solely with vital wheat gluten. Look for chickpea flour in natural food stores.

Chipotle chiles in adobo sauce, canned. When smoke-dried, jalapeño chiles are known as chipotle chiles. Their spicy, smoky flavor is wonderful for enhancing soups, stews, and other dishes. Although chipotle chiles are available dried, you'll want to keep canned chipotle chiles in adobo sauce on hand because several of the recipes in this book call for them. Look for canned chipotle chiles in adobo sauce with the Mexican or Latin American foods in most supermarkets.

Chocolate chips. Though not all semisweet chocolate chips are vegan, many generic supermarket brands are free of dairy products. Natural food stores also sell vegan chocolate chips, but you might save a buck by buying generic chips at conventional grocery stores.

Cider vinegar. Cider vinegar is my go-to vinegar for making vegan buttermilk for use in biscuits, cornbread, and other baked goods. Just add 1 to 2 teaspoons to 1 cup of soy milk and let it stand for 2 minutes to curdle and thicken.

Confectioners' sugar. Also called powdered sugar, confectioners' sugar is a very fine white sugar that's essential for creating creamy frostings.

Cornstarch. Many of my recipes call for cornstarch as a thickener in place of eggs or flour. Arrowroot starch, a thickener made from the root of a tropical plant, may be substituted, but I prefer cornstarch because it's widely available and more affordable.

Cream of mushroom soup. A few recipes in this book call for creamy vegan mushroom soup. I've provided a recipe for making your own from scratch in the chapter Soup's On (page 68). But if you want to save time, I recommend using Imagine Foods brand creamy mushroom soup.

Ener-G egg replacer. Various brands of powdered egg replacers are available, but each uses a different amount of the powder and water to equal one egg. I tested these recipes using Ener-G egg replacer, which is perfect for replacing eggs in cakes, pies, and cookies. Look for it at natural food stores or in the natural food section of your supermarket, or order it online.

Flaxseeds, ground. Ground flaxseeds mixed with a little water do a great job of binding ingredients together—something eggs often do in batters for baked goods. Plus, they offer a nice boost of essential omega-3 fatty acids. Since the ground seeds tend to be grainy, I only use flaxseeds to replace eggs in heartier desserts and breads. The recipes in this book specify quantities of flaxseeds and water to use, but if you want to try this substitution in other recipes, use 1 tablespoon of ground flaxseeds to 3 tablespoons of hot water to equal each egg. If you buy whole flaxseeds, grind them in a coffee grinder and store them in a sealed container in the refrigerator or freezer for up to one month. Flaxseeds that are stored in the freezer don't need to be thawed before using.

Greek seasoning salt. Once you've made a few recipes from this book, you'll probably notice that I'm a big fan of seasoning salts. One of my favorites is Greek seasoning salt, a blend of black pepper, garlic, onion, oregano, and other spices. My go-to brand of Greek seasoning is Cavender's, which can be found in supermarkets or online at cavendersseasoning.com. If you don't have Greek seasoning, substitute any all-purpose seasoning salt.

Hoisin sauce. The complex salty-sweet flavor of hoisin sauce, a Chinese dipping sauce made from soybeans, vinegar, garlic, and chiles, is a key ingredient in several of the marinades in this book. Look for it in Asian supermarkets or the ethnic-foods aisle in mainstream grocery stores.

Jalapeño chiles. A great way to dial up the heat level in dishes is with fresh jalapeño chiles. I'm a big fan of spicy foods, so I use them seeds and all. If you prefer fresh chile flavor with less of a kick, remove the seeds and membranes. Also, note that the oils in chiles can burn your skin. Try to minimize the amount you handle them, and if your skin is sensitive, you might want to wear gloves. Most of all, wash your hands well after handling chiles and be careful not to touch your eyes or other sensitive areas for a while afterward.

Liquid smoke. A must-have for every vegan cook, liquid smoke imparts, well, a smoky flavor to marinades and sauces, and it's a perfect stand-in for the flavor bacon contributes to traditional slow-cooked collard greens.

Nutritional yeast. The key ingredient in vegan cheese sauces, nutritional yeast is made from deactivated yeast and boasts a nutty, cheesy flavor. Fondly referred to as "nooch" by some vegans, fortified nutritional yeast (such as KAL brand) is also a good vegan source of vitamin B_{12}, a nutrient that's often in short supply in vegan diets.

Pasta. I only use whole wheat or whole-grain pastas. If you can find quinoa macaroni, it's a terrific alternative to regular semolina macaroni, since it's similar in taste, color, and texture. Whole wheat spaghetti and penne are also delicious—and more nutritious than white pasta.

Peanut butter, natural. I recommend using only natural peanut butters free of hydrogenated oils. The oil in natural nut butters tends to separate when the jar sits on the shelf for very long, so be sure to stir it before each use.

Pecans. Native to the south-central United States, pecans are a natural in Southern cooking. Opt for raw pecan halves and store them in the freezer for maximum freshness. Oh, and for the record, in the South, we pronounce pecan in a way that rhymes with "Dijon." You won't hear folks down here saying "pee-can."

Poultry seasoning. You can buy poultry seasoning, which is usually used to season stuffings, in the spice aisle at the grocery store, but you may already have all the herbs needed to make your own at home. Just combine 2 teaspoons of rubbed sage, $1/2$ teaspoon of dried thyme, and $1/2$ teaspoon of dried marjoram. Once you've mixed them together, store the unused portion in a small airtight jar.

Seasoning salt. Many recipes in this book call for various seasoning-salt blends—adobo seasoning, Cajun seasoning, and Greek seasoning salt—and some just call for plain ol' seasoning salt. Experiment with different varieties and brands, and feel free to substitute your favorite in any recipe.

Seitan. Made from wheat gluten, seitan is a hearty, chewy, protein-rich food that works beautifully as a stand-in for meat in conventional dishes. You can make your own seitan using the recipes in this book (see the recipe for Seitan Chicken on page 16 and the recipe for Seitan Ribs on page 96), or you can buy packaged seitan at natural food stores. Look for it in the refrigerated section.

Sorghum syrup. Sorghum syrup, made from the sweet sorghum plant, is a common sweetener down South, but it may not be easy to find in other parts of the United States. Blackstrap molasses, a by-product of the sugarcane industry, is similar in taste and texture and may be substituted for sorghum syrup in any of the recipes in this book. Both are rich in minerals. Also, note that sorghum syrup may be labeled "sorghum molasses."

Soy milk. I recommend soy milk over other nondairy milks, so that's what I call for in most of my recipes. I haven't had much luck curdling other nondairy milks when making vegan buttermilk for baked goods and breads, so I stick with soy milk. However, other nondairy milks, such as almond, coconut, or hemp milk, may be substituted in recipes that don't require curdling. When using any type of nondairy milk in savory recipes, note that those labeled "plain" may contain sugar, so be sure to select a variety labeled "unsweetened."

Soy sauce. I tend to use soy sauce instead of the supposedly more healthful alternatives, like tamari, shoyu, and Bragg Liquid Aminos. For me, that's strictly an economical decision, since soy sauce tends to be more affordable. Plus, the quantities used are usually fairly small. Feel free to substitute tamari, shoyu, or Bragg Liquid Aminos for soy sauce in any of my recipes.

Sriracha sauce. If I were stranded on a desert island with only one condiment, I'd choose sriracha sauce. This sweet-hot Thai chili sauce offers a more complex flavor than vinegar-based hot sauces. I put it on almost everything. Look for it in Asian markets or in the ethnic aisle at well-stocked supermarkets.

Sugar. I only buy evaporated cane juice, but I refer to it as "sugar" in my recipes because white sugar, which is more widely available (and affordable), will work just fine. Evaporated cane juice is less processed than white sugar, so some of the sugarcane's nutrients are retained. Seek out evaporated cane juice if you can find it. It's usually available at natural food stores.

Tahini. The signature ingredient in hummus, tahini is simply a paste made by grinding sesame seeds. It has a high calcium content and a healthy dose of healthful fats. It's available in roasted and raw varieties. Feel free to use either one in my recipes.

Tempeh. Originally from Indonesia, tempeh is a fermented soy product that boasts high amounts of protein and fiber. It tends to have a bitter flavor, so I recommend steaming it for 10 minutes before using it in a recipe; this tends to remove any bitterness.

Textured soy protein (TSP). TSP is a meat substitute made from defatted soy flour. It's high in protein, low in fat, and extremely versatile, since it soaks up flavors like a sponge. It comes in dry form—in sizes ranging from small crumbles similar to the texture of ground beef to chunky pieces along the lines of beef tips. It must be rehydrated in boiling water or broth before use.

Tofu, silken. The most widely available brand of silken tofu is Mori-Nu, which is sold in 12.3-ounce shelf-stable aseptic packages, but you may be able to find other brands of silken tofu (usually in 14- to 16-ounce tubs) in the produce section or with other refrigerated natural foods. Use it for making creamy sauces and dressings.

Tofu, extra-firm regular. Although regular tofu comes in soft, firm, and extra-firm varieties, I only use extra-firm tofu in my recipes. Pressing this tofu for thirty minutes, either with heavy objects or a tofu press, gives it an even firmer texture. To press it, put the block of tofu on a plate or rimmed baking sheet. Put a second plate or baking sheet on top and place a heavy object on top, like a heavy skillet or a big can of tomatoes. Be sure to center the weight over the tofu, and don't use so much weight that you squash the tofu. Press for fifteen to thirty minutes.

Vegan cheese. The taste and texture of vegan cheese has improved dramatically in recent years. It may be sold in shredded, sliced, or block form and is available in most natural foods stores and with the natural foods in well-stocked supermarkets. Be sure to check the ingredients in nondairy cheeses to make sure they don't contain casein, a milk protein used in some soy- and rice-based cheeses. To streamline your search, I can recommend two brands: Daiya and Follow Your Heart Vegan Gourmet.

Vegan margarine. Opt for nonhydrogenated vegan margarines, which are more healthful than hydrogenated varieties. I prefer Earth Balance buttery spreads and sticks, which are made with all-natural ingredients.

Vegan mayonnaise. There are several brands of vegan mayo available in natural food stores, and all are similar to conventional mayonnaise in both taste and texture. I also provide a recipe for Tofu Mayo on page 8, as a more affordable alternative. If you're feelin' lazy, the store-bought brands I recommend are Follow Your Heart Vegenaise and Earth Balance MindfulMayo.

Vegan sausage. Some vegetarian sausage patties contain eggs, but vegan versions are available. I recommend using Gimme Lean, a vegan sausage sold in tubes, rather than frozen patties; just slice and fry it before using it in any recipes in this book that call for sausage patties.

Vegan Worcestershire sauce. Conventional Worcestershire sauce contains anchovies, so I provide a recipe to make a vegan version from scratch on page 10. You can also buy vegan Worcestershire sauce at natural food stores, but it's pretty spendy.

Vegetable broth. It's easy to make rich, flavorful homemade vegetable broth. Just save and freeze vegetable scraps, such as celery tops, pepper ends, carrot bits, and so on. The only veggie scraps to avoid are onion skins and those from cruciferous vegetables, as they can impart a strong, bitter taste. When you have enough scraps to fill a stockpot at least halfway, put them in the pot, add water to cover the vegetables, and bring to a boil. Cover and simmer for about 1 hour, then strain out the vegetables and freeze the broth in 1-cup portions. Of course, you can also use store-bought vegetable broth if you want to save time.

Vegetable shortening. Although most conventional brands of vegetable shortening are vegan, many are made with nasty hydrogenated oils. Opt for nonhydrogenated vegetable shortening, which you can find at natural food stores and some conventional supermarkets.

Vital wheat gluten. The key ingredient in homemade seitan, vital wheat gluten can usually be found in the bulk bins at natural food stores or in the baking aisle at most conventional grocery stores.

Whole wheat pastry flour. Whole wheat pastry flour is less processed than all-purpose white flour, making it a wiser choice for optimum nutrition. Pastry flour has a softer texture than regular whole wheat flour, so it can be substituted for all-purpose flour in most recipes. I call for whole wheat pastry flour in most of my recipes, with the exception of cakes and cupcakes. Through trial and error, I've learned that whole wheat pastry flour makes for dense cakes, so I recommend using unbleached all-purpose flour for those.

JUST THE BASICS

CONDIMENTS, SAUCES, AND FAUX MEATS

This chapter features recipes for ingredients called for in other chapters of the book. You'll find a creamy vegan buttermilk ranch dressing, a tofu-based mayo, and my favorite tahini sauce, which is great for toppin' salads or spreadin' on sandwiches. Of course, I've also included my tried-and-true recipe for a smoky Memphis-style 'cue sauce, characterized by a strong vinegar flavor paired with sweet molasses and maple syrup. This sauce is featured in numerous recipes throughout the book, and while you're welcome to cheat with a store-bought sauce, once you taste my version you won't mind spendin' just a bit of time to make it from scratch.

This chapter also contains recipes for several faux meats, including marinated tofu chicken and a ground beef analog using textured soy protein, and an easy method for making and flavoring seitan at home. If you keep various preparations from this chapter on hand, you'll be able to throw together a satisfying Southern meal with minimal muss and fuss.

This light and creamy mayonnaise substitute is an affordable alternative to store-bought vegan mayo. Spread it on sandwiches or use it as a dressing for White-Trash Pineapple Salad (page 51).

Tofu Mayo

1½ cups crumbled firm silken tofu

2 tablespoons extra-virgin olive oil

1 tablespoon freshly squeezed lemon juice

1 teaspoon agave nectar

¼ teaspoon salt

Put all the ingredients in a food processor. Process until smooth and creamy, stopping occasionally to scrape down the work bowl and move the mixture toward the blades. Stored in a sealed container in the refrigerator, Tofu Mayo will keep for 5 days.

Per 2 tablespoons: 53 calories, 3 g protein, 4 g fat (1 g sat), 2 g carbs, 68 mg sodium, 13 mg calcium, 0 g fiber

**N**othing compares to a big ol' garden salad covered in creamy ranch dressing. This homemade vegan version boasts a thick, creamy texture reminiscent of those non-vegan dips made with packets of dry seasoning and sour cream. There are many ways to enjoy this dressing, including atop BBQ Seitan Salad (page 57) or as a dip for Fried Cucumbers (page 131) or Spicy Seitan Hot Wangs (page 93).

Country Buttermilk Ranch Dressing

MAKES ABOUT ²/₃ CUP

2 tablespoons unsweetened soy milk

¼ teaspoon cider vinegar

½ cup vegan sour cream

½ teaspoon onion powder

¼ teaspoon dried dill weed

¼ teaspoon salt

¼ teaspoon garlic powder

Put the soy milk and vinegar in a small bowl and stir well. Set aside until the soy milk curdles and thickens, about 2 minutes.

Put the vegan sour cream, onion powder, dill weed, salt, and garlic powder in a medium bowl and mix well. Add the soy milk mixture and stir until thoroughly blended. Stored in a sealed container in the refrigerator, Country Buttermilk Ranch Dressing will keep for 1 week.

NOTE: For a thinner salad dressing, add a little more soy milk.

RANCH DIP: To make a ranch dip for fresh vegetables, omit the soy milk and vinegar.

Per 2 tablespoons: 50 calories, 1 g protein, 4 g fat (4 g sat), 2 g carbs, 132 mg sodium, 3 mg calcium, 0 g fiber

Traditional Worcestershire sauce contains anchovies. A fish-free vegan version is available at most natural food stores. But you can make your own with this recipe, which uses common pantry items, if you don't have access to a natural food store or you're lookin' to save a few bucks. Use this sauce in Tangy Tempeh Chops with Green Peppers (page 92), Sweet 'n' Sour Bean Balls (page 43), or various other recipes in this book. It's also a great seasoning for Bloody Marys.

Vegan Worcestershire Sauce

MAKES ABOUT ¾ CUP

½ cup reduced-sodium soy sauce

¼ cup cider vinegar

2 tablespoons blackstrap molasses

1 tablespoon brown sugar

½ teaspoon onion powder

¼ teaspoon ground allspice

¼ teaspoon dry mustard

¼ teaspoon liquid smoke

⅛ teaspoon cayenne

⅛ teaspoon ground cloves

⅛ teaspoon garlic powder

Put all the ingredients in a small saucepan and mix well. Bring to a boil over medium heat. Decrease the heat to low and cook, stirring occasionally, for 15 minutes.

Let cool, then store in a sealed container in the refrigerator, where the sauce will keep for about 3 months. Stir or shake vigorously before each use.

Per tablespoon: 20 calories, 1 g protein, 0 g fat (0 g sat), 5 g carbs, 336 mg sodium, 30 mg calcium, 0 g fiber

se this calcium-rich creamy sauce in Protein Power Pockets (page 62), as a dip for fresh veggies, or for toppin' cooked kale or collard greens.

Creamy Tahini Sauce

⅓ cup tahini

2 tablespoons freshly squeezed lemon juice

2 tablespoons nutritional yeast

1 tablespoon toasted sesame oil

1 tablespoon reduced-sodium soy sauce

1 tablespoon maple syrup

¼ teaspoon garlic powder

Put all the ingredients in a blender and process until smooth. Alternatively, put all the ingredients in a small bowl and whisk vigorously or beat with a fork until smooth.

TAHINI SALAD DRESSING: To use this sauce as a salad dressing, thin it with 1 to 2 tablespoons of water.

Per 2 tablespoons: 129 calories, 4 g protein, 10 g fat (1 g sat), 7 g carbs, 112 mg sodium, 66 mg calcium, 2 g fiber

Memphis, the city I call home, is the barbecue capital of the world. Others may try to claim that coveted title, but no region's 'cue can match that of the Bluff City. Memphis is even home to the World Championship Barbecue Cooking Contest, an annual three-day competition of the world's top pit masters. Luckily for vegans (and for animals), the secret to barbecue is in the sauce. In addition to using it as a marinade for grilled tofu or tempeh, you can slather it on anything from veggie burgers to French fries.

Memphis-Style Barbecue Sauce

MAKES 1 CUP

1 cup ketchup

¼ cup cider vinegar

3 tablespoons maple syrup

2 tablespoons blackstrap molasses

1 tablespoon reduced-sodium
　soy sauce

½ teaspoon liquid smoke

¼ teaspoon dry mustard

¼ teaspoon onion powder

⅛ teaspoon garlic powder

Put all the ingredients in a small saucepan and mix well. Cook over medium-high heat, stirring occasionally, until steaming but not boiling. Decrease the heat to low and cook, stirring occasionally, until slightly thickened and the flavors have blended, 15 minutes.

Let cool, then store in a sealed container in the refrigerator, where the sauce will keep for 2 weeks.

Per 2 tablespoons: 66 calories, 0 g protein, 0 g fat (0 g sat), 16 g carbs, 466 mg sodium, 49 mg calcium, 0 g fiber

ere's a bare-bones recipe for an easy cheesy sauce made with nutritional yeast. Stir this sauce into cooked pasta for a quick vegan mac and cheese, or use it to make Cheesy Broccoli-Rice Casserole (page 111). Spread it on veggie burgers, or stir in some salsa for nacho cheese dip. These are just a few of the many possibilities. If you're just cooking for one, feel free to cut the recipe in half, but you might find the sauce to be such a useful staple that you'll want to make a full batch so you always have some on hand.

Basic Cheesy Sauce

MAKES 3 CUPS

1½ cups nutritional yeast

½ cup whole wheat pastry flour

1 teaspoon garlic powder

½ teaspoon salt, plus more if desired

1½ cups unsweetened soy milk

1½ cups water

2 tablespoons nonhydrogenated
vegan margarine

2 teaspoons Dijon mustard

Put the nutritional yeast, flour, garlic powder, and salt in a medium saucepan and mix well. Add the soy milk and water and whisk until thoroughly blended. Cook over medium heat, whisking constantly, until thickened, about 7 minutes. Remove from the heat and stir in the margarine and mustard. Taste and add more salt if desired.

SPICY CHEESY SAUCE: Add 4 teaspoons of sriracha sauce when stirring in the vegan margarine and mustard.

Per ¼ cup: 77 calories, 5 g protein, 3 g fat (1 g sat), 8 g carbs, 144 mg sodium, 10 mg calcium, 2 g fiber

his all-purpose marinated tofu is the perfect filling for Protein Power Pockets (page 62) or Fried Green Tomato and Tofu Sandwiches (page 63). The method here calls for cutting the tofu into slabs and baking it, but you can also cut it into bite-sized cubes and use it in a stir-fry. Another option is tossing it on the grill at your next barbecue party. If you do that, you might want to cut the tofu into thicker slabs than called for in this recipe.

Sweet 'n' Spicy Marinated Tofu

Advance preparation required

MAKES 4 TO 8 HELPIN'S

1 pound extra-firm regular tofu, drained and pressed (see page 5)

1 cup low-sodium vegetable broth

½ cup reduced-sodium soy sauce

1 tablespoon extra-virgin olive oil

1 tablespoon maple syrup

1 teaspoon liquid smoke

1 to 2 teaspoons sriracha sauce

2 cloves garlic, minced

Slice the tofu into 8 equal slabs.

Put the broth, soy sauce, oil, maple syrup, liquid smoke, 1 teaspoon of the sriracha sauce, and the garlic in a large, shallow storage container. Whisk until thoroughly blended. Taste and add more sriracha sauce if desired.

Put the tofu in the container and gently flip the slabs over to evenly coat them with the marinade. Cover and refrigerate for 8 to 12 hours, gently turning the tofu once or twice during the marinating time.

Preheat the oven to 375 degrees F. Spray a baking sheet with cooking spray or line it with parchment paper.

Remove the tofu from the marinade and put the slices on the prepared baking sheet. Discard the marinade. Bake for 30 minutes, until lightly browned, carefully flipping the tofu halfway through the baking time.

SWEET 'N' SAVORY MARINATED TOFU: Substitute 1 teaspoon of ground ginger for the sriracha sauce.

Per serving (based on 6 servings): 102 calories, 10 g protein, 5 g fat (1 g sat), 5 g carbs, 364 mg sodium, 136 mg calcium, 1 g fiber

This tofu can be used interchangeably with Sweet 'n' Spicy Marinated Tofu (page 14). Unbaked, it's also a key ingredient in several recipes in this book: Southern Fried Tofu Chicken (page 90), Cornmeal-Crusted Tofu Stix (page 91), and Creamy Tofu Chicken Pasta Bake (page 114). Other options for using it include cutting the tofu into bite-sized cubes before marinating and then putting it in a stir-fry, or cutting the tofu into thick slabs and, once marinated, cooking it on a grill.

Tofu Chicken

Advance preparation required   MAKES 4 TO 8 HELPIN'S

1 pound extra-firm regular tofu, drained and pressed (see page 5)

1 cup low-sodium vegetable broth

½ cup water

2 tablespoons nutritional yeast

2 tablespoons reduced-sodium soy sauce

1 teaspoon onion powder

1 teaspoon adobo seasoning or seasoning salt

½ teaspoon poultry seasoning

Slice the tofu into 8 equal slabs or cut it into the size and shape specified in the recipe it's to be used in (see note).

Put the broth, water, nutritional yeast, soy sauce, onion powder, adobo seasoning, and poultry seasoning in a large, shallow storage container. Whisk until thoroughly blended.

Put the tofu in the container and gently flip the slabs over to evenly coat them with the marinade. Cover and refrigerate for 8 to 12 hours, gently turning the tofu once or twice during the marinating time.

Preheat the oven to 375 degrees F. Spray a baking sheet with cooking spray or line it with parchment paper.

Remove the tofu from the marinade and put the slices on the prepared baking sheet. Discard the marinade. Bake for 30 minutes, until lightly browned, carefully flipping the tofu halfway through the baking time.

NOTE: If using the Tofu Chicken in Southern Fried Tofu Chicken (page 90), cut it into 8 slabs, as directed here. To use it in Cornmeal-Crusted Tofu Stix (page 91), slice the tofu into 8 equal sticks. If using it in Creamy Tofu Chicken Pasta Bake (page 114), cut the tofu into bite-sized cubes.

Per serving (based on 6 servings): 85 calories, 9 g protein, 4 g fat (1 g sat), 3 g carbs, 214 mg sodium, 135 mg calcium, 1 g fiber

Praise seitan! This wheat gluten meat substitute is packed with protein and has a meatier texture than tofu or tempeh. You can buy premade seitan at most natural food stores, but it's more economical (and tastier) to make it yourself. My version is different from most of the recipes you'll see for seitan, as it includes some chickpea flour.

Seitan Chicken

MAKES ABOUT 3 CUPS

SEITAN DOUGH

1 cup vital wheat gluten

⅓ cup chickpea flour (see notes)

¼ cup nutritional yeast

½ teaspoon adobo seasoning or seasoning salt

1 cup water

FAUX CHICKEN BROTH

2¾ cups water

¼ cup nutritional yeast

1 tablespoon reduced-sodium soy sauce

2 teaspoons onion powder

1 teaspoon poultry seasoning

¼ teaspoon celery salt

To make the dough, put the vital wheat gluten, chickpea flour, nutritional yeast, and adobo seasoning in a medium bowl and mix well. Stir in the water, then knead the dough in the bowl for 5 minutes. It will be very wet at first, but as you knead, it will thicken and become quite firm. Let the dough rest for 5 minutes.

To make the faux chicken broth, put all the ingredients in a large pot and mix well. Bring to a boil over high heat.

To cook the seitan, tear the dough into chunks of the desired size (see notes), dropping the chunks into the boiling broth as you go. Seitan expands as it cooks, so the pieces of dough should be smaller than the final size desired.

Let the broth return to a boil after adding all of the dough. Decrease the heat to medium-low, cover, and cook, stirring occasionally, until most of the liquid is absorbed, about 45 minutes.

Scoop the seitan out of the broth using a slotted spoon if you plan to use it immediately, or store the seitan in any extra broth in the refrigerator or freezer until ready to use. Discard any liquid before using. Stored in a sealed container, cooked seitan will keep for about 1 week in the refrigerator or about 3 months in the freezer.

Per ½ cup: 120 calories, 19 g protein, 1 g fat (0 g sat), 9 g carbs, 269 mg sodium, 49 mg calcium, 2 g fiber

This addition gives the seitan a more tender texture. Once you're done with the kneading, simmer the seitan chunks in faux chicken broth, as in the main recipe, or faux beef broth, as in the variation. Seitan Chicken is great to have on hand for a variety of dishes in this book, including Dijon-Pecan Seitan with Maple-Mustard Glaze (page 100) and Seitan and Root Veggie Potpie (page 115).

SEITAN BEEF: To make beef-flavored seitan, which is used in Seitan Tips over Brown Rice (page 97) and Seitan Beef Stew (page 98), substitute a faux beef broth for the faux chicken broth. To make the faux beef broth, combine 1¾ cups water, 1 cup vegetable broth, ¼ cup soy sauce, 2 tablespoons vegan Worcestershire sauce (homemade, page 10, or store-bought), and 1 teaspoon onion powder. Follow the instructions in the main recipe for boiling the broth and cooking the seitan.

NOTES

- You can substitute whole wheat pastry flour for the chickpea flour, but the seitan will be softer.
- If using the seitan in a recipe in this book, consult that recipe to see what size the chunks should be. A size that works well in most of the recipes in this book is ½- to 1-inch pieces.

ou can buy frozen ground veggie burger crumbles, but textured soy protein (TSP), available in the bulk bins at natural food stores, is more economical. Use TSP in any recipe that calls for veggie burger crumbles (or ground beef), such as chili, spaghetti, Cheesy Burger Mac (page 85), or Hungry Jill Casserole (page 116).

Ground TSP Beef

MAKES 1 CUP

1½ cups water

¼ cup reduced-sodium soy sauce

2 teaspoons onion powder

2 teaspoons vegan Worcestershire sauce (homemade, page 10, or store-bought)

1 cup dry TSP crumbles (see page 5)

Put the water, soy sauce, onion powder, and Worcestershire sauce in a medium saucepan and mix well. Bring to a boil over high heat. Stir in the TSP crumbles. Decrease the heat to medium-low, cover, and cook, stirring occasionally, until most of the liquid is absorbed, 20 to 25 minutes. Drain in a fine-mesh sieve.

Per ¼ cup: 82 calories, 12 g protein, 0 g fat (0 g sat), 9 g carbs, 562 mg sodium, 59 mg calcium, 2 g fiber

everal years ago, the lovely Julie Hasson of Everyday Dish TV made the world's greatest contribution to vegan cuisine: the steamed vegan sausage. These tasty sausages, which have a vital wheat gluten base, offer authentic texture and flavor, yet they're low in fat. Her original recipe, posted all over the vegan blogosphere, leant itself to creative substitutions. I've taken the basics and added my own N'awlins-inspired flavors for a spicy sausage that is an excellent brunch side dish, a wonderful accompaniment to Cheesy Tofu Scramble (page 30), and an ideal ingredient in Eggplant and Creole Sausage Jambalaya (page 102).

Creole Steamed Sausages

MAKES 8 SAUSAGES; 6 TO 8 HELPIN'S

½ cup canned Great Northern beans, drained and rinsed

1 cup low-sodium vegetable broth

3 cloves garlic, minced

1 tablespoon rubbed sage

1 tablespoon extra-virgin olive oil

1 tablespoon reduced-sodium soy sauce

1 tablespoon sriracha sauce or other hot sauce

1½ teaspoons smoked paprika

1 teaspoon Cajun seasoning

1 teaspoon liquid smoke

1 teaspoon dried thyme

½ teaspoon cayenne

1¼ cups vital wheat gluten

Cut eight squares of aluminum foil that measure about 10 inches square.

Put the beans in a large bowl and mash with a potato masher or a fork until fairly smooth. Add the broth, garlic, sage, oil, soy sauce, sriracha sauce, paprika, Cajun seasoning, liquid smoke, thyme, and cayenne and mix well.

Stir in the vital wheat gluten, then knead the dough in the bowl for 5 minutes. It will be very wet at first, but as you knead, it will thicken and become quite firm. Let the dough rest for 5 minutes.

Divide the dough into 8 equal pieces and shape them into balls. Roll each ball between your palms to form a sausage. Lay a sausage along the lower edge of one of the squares of aluminum foil. Roll the sausage up tightly in the foil, then twist the ends (like a hard-candy wrapper) to seal. Repeat with the remaining pieces of dough.

Steam the sausages for 40 minutes, checking periodically to make sure the water in the steamer doesn't get too low. If it does, add more hot water and continue steaming. If your steamer isn't large, it's fine to stack the sausages on top of each other.

Let the sausages cool slightly before unwrapping them. Stored in a sealed container or ziplock bag, the steamed sausages will keep for about 5 days in the refrigerator or 3 months in the freezer.

NOTE: If you're not using the sausages in a recipe, try frying them up whole or sliced in a skillet sprayed with a little cooking spray or lightly coated with oil.

Per sausage: 110 calories, 16 g protein, 2 g fat (0 g sat), 7 g carbs, 184 mg sodium, 51 mg calcium, 1 g fiber

GRITS, GRAVIES, AND SUCH

BIG OL' SOUTHERN BREAKFASTS

Quick breakfasts of cereal or oatmeal are fine for a rushed weekday mornin' meal, but why not celebrate the weekend with a great big Southern breakfast? In this chapter, you'll mostly find recipes fit for a lazy Saturday morning or late Sunday brunch.

There's nothing more satisfying than starting the day with an overstuffed platter of Cheesy Tempeh Bacon Grits (page 26), Brown Sugar–Baked Tofu Ham with Redeye Gravy (page 33), and fluffy Whole Wheat Buttermilk Biscuits (page 136) with luscious Chocolate Gravy (page 23). With a meal like that under your belt, you're guaranteed to stay full through lunchtime. Not a big breakfast eater? Try these recipes for a down-home "brinner" (that means breakfast for dinner) or single out one dish for a heartier weekday breakfast.

Back in my prevegan days, chunky dairy cottage cheese was pure comfort food. I'd eat it straight out of the tub or accompanied by fresh fruit or toast. I've tried several different recipes for vegan cottage cheese, and although all have been pretty decent, this version stands out as the most satisfying. I like to spread it on whole wheat toast with Marmite, a salty, savory British yeast spread.

Tofu Cottage Cheese

YIELDS 2 CUPS; 4 TO 6 HELPIN'S

1 pound extra-firm regular tofu, drained and pressed (see page 5)

¼ cup sweetened plain nondairy yogurt

1 tablespoon vegan mayonnaise or Tofu Mayo (page 8)

Pinch salt

Crumble the tofu into a large bowl, aiming for chunks about the size of the curds in dairy cottage cheese. Add the nondairy yogurt, vegan mayonnaise, and salt and mix well. Refrigerate until ready to serve.

Per serving (based on 5 servings): 109 calories, 11 g protein, 5 g fat (1 g sat), 4 g carbs, 16 mg sodium, 181 mg calcium, 1 g fiber

Clockwise from top: **Cheesy Tempeh Bacon Grits,** *page 26;* **Whole Wheat Buttermilk Biscuit,** *page 136,* **topped with Chocolate Gravy,** *page 23;* **Country-Fried Tempeh Steak,** *page 94,* **with Whole Wheat Buttermilk Biscuits,** *page 136,* **and Sausage Gravy with Sage,** *page 24*

Jalapeño-Lime Watermelon Salad, *page 48*

ou haven't had a true Southern breakfast until you've tried chocolate gravy over biscuits. Ironically, I first sampled this rich sauce on a family trip to Indiana, but a lady with Arkansas roots prepared it. Spoon this gravy liberally over Whole Wheat Buttermilk Biscuits (page 136). It's like eating dessert for breakfast!

Chocolate Gravy

See photo facing page 22.

YIELDS 1 CUP; 3 TO 4 HELPIN'S

1 cup plain soy milk

1 teaspoon vanilla extract

½ cup sugar

2 tablespoons whole wheat pastry flour

2 tablespoons unsweetened cocoa powder

1 tablespoon nonhydrogenated vegan margarine

Put the soy milk and vanilla extract in a small bowl and mix well.

Put the sugar, flour, and cocoa powder in a medium bowl and mix well. Pour in the soy milk mixture and stir until the sugar is dissolved.

Melt the margarine in a small saucepan over medium heat. Add the soy milk mixture and cook, stirring constantly, until the gravy thickens, 7 to 10 minutes. Remove from the heat. Serve immediately.

Per serving (based on 3.5 servings): 200 calories, 4 g protein, 5 g fat (1 g sat), 35 g carbs, 65 mg sodium, 27 mg calcium, 2 g fiber

his creamy gravy recipe is totally low-fat! But it's so rich tasting that if I hadn't told you, you'd never know it. When developing this recipe, I forgot to add oil, a staple in traditional Southern milk gravy. Turns out it tasted just fine without the fat. This gravy is perfect for pourin' over Whole Wheat Buttermilk Biscuits (page 136).

Sausage Gravy with Sage

See photo facing page 22.

YIELDS ABOUT 2 CUPS; 4 TO 8 HELPIN'S

7 ounces (one-half tube) **Gimme Lean Sausage**

⅓ cup whole wheat pastry flour

1 teaspoon rubbed sage

½ teaspoon onion powder

2 cups unsweetened soy milk

½ teaspoon salt

Ground pepper

Slice the vegan sausage into 5 or 6 patties. Spray a medium skillet with cooking spray. Put the skillet over medium heat, add the patties, and cook until brown on the bottom, 3 to 4 minutes. Flip the patties and cook until brown on the other side, about 3 minutes. Transfer to a plate and break into bite-sized pieces with a fork.

Put the flour, sage, onion powder, soy milk, and salt in a medium saucepan and whisk until well mixed and lump-free. Cook over medium heat, stirring constantly with the whisk, until the mixture thickens, 7 to 10 minutes. Remove from the heat and stir in the vegan sausage. Season with pepper to taste. Serve immediately.

Per serving (based on 6 servings): 105 calories, 9 g protein, 2 g fat (0 g sat), 13 g carbs, 393 mg sodium, 50 mg calcium, 3 g fiber

outhern omnivores worship bacon, eating it for breakfast, on sandwiches, and in salads. They even put it in their greens and soup beans. You'll be glad to know this cruelty-free bacon can be used in all the same ways.

Bringin' Home the Tempeh Bacon

Advance preparation required   **YIELDS 10 TO 12 STRIPS; 5 TO 6 HELPIN'S**

8 ounces tempeh, sliced lengthwise into 10 to 12 strips

1 cup low-sodium vegetable broth

½ cup reduced-sodium soy sauce

2 tablespoons hoisin sauce

2 tablespoons maple syrup

2 teaspoons liquid smoke

Steam the tempeh for 10 minutes.

Put the broth, soy sauce, hoisin sauce, maple syrup, and liquid smoke in a large, shallow storage container. Whisk until thoroughly blended.

Put the tempeh in the container and gently flip the strips over to evenly coat them with the marinade. Cover and refrigerate for 8 to 12 hours, turning the tempeh once or twice during the marinating time.

Preheat the oven to 400 degrees F. Spray a baking sheet with cooking spray or line it with parchment paper.

Drain the tempeh in a colander. Put the slices on the prepared baking sheet. Bake for 20 minutes, until crispy and the edges are brown, carefully flipping the tempeh halfway through the baking time.

Per 2 strips (based on 11 strips): 102 calories, 9 g protein, 4 g fat (1 g sat), 7 g carbs, 437 mg sodium, 50 mg calcium, 2 g fiber

I t doesn't get more Southern than a steaming bowl of buttery, cheesy grits at the breakfast table. We like 'em so much down here, we even eat them for lunch and dinner. Enjoy these cheesy bacon-flavored grits mornin', noon, and night.

Cheesy Tempeh Bacon Grits

See photo facing page 22.

Advance preparation required   **YIELDS 4 HELPIN'S**

2½ cups water

1 cup unsweetened soy milk, plus more if needed

1 tablespoon nonhydrogenated vegan margarine

1 teaspoon onion powder

1 teaspoon salt

Ground pepper

1 cup yellow corn grits (see notes)

5 to 6 slices (4 ounces) **Bringin' Home the Tempeh Bacon** (page 25), crumbled

½ cup shredded vegan Cheddar cheese (optional)

6 tablespoons nutritional yeast

Put 1½ cups of the water and the soy milk, margarine, onion powder, salt, and as much pepper as desired in a medium saucepan and mix well. Bring to a boil over medium-high heat. Decrease the heat to low, then whisk in the grits. Cook, stirring occasionally, until the grits begin to thicken, 5 to 7 minutes. Stir in the remaining cup of water. Cover and cook, stirring occasionally, until the water is absorbed and the grits are thick, creamy, and tender, about 10 minutes (see notes). Remove from the heat.

Stir in the tempeh bacon, optional vegan cheese, and nutritional yeast. If the grits seem too dry, stir in more soy milk, 1 tablespoon at a time, to achieve the desired consistency.

NOTES

- Grits are a Southern breakfast staple sold as a ground meal. I only use yellow corn grits since they're made from whole corn kernels, whereas some white grits are made from hulled corn, hominy, or naturally white corn. Feel free to substitute white grits, but look for a variety made with whole white corn if you can find it.

- Grits can be a little tricky to prepare. Sometimes they thicken up before they're good and tender. Long cooking over low heat and a watchful eye are key to cookin' up perfect grits. Don't step away from the stove for too long, or they might get too thick and burn. With a little practice, you'll be a pro at cookin' grits in no time.

- If you plan on making the grits several hours before serving, you'll need to add a few splashes of soy milk before reheating on the stove or in the microwave. Grits firm up after cooling, but including a little extra liquid when reheating makes them creamy again.

Per serving: 274 calories, 14 g protein, 8 g fat (2 g sat), 39 g carbs, 889 mg sodium, 55 mg calcium, 5 g fiber

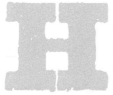ere's a more healthful variation of corned beef hash, a Southern breakfast staple. Start the day off right by trading the corned beef for crumbled veggie burgers and the white potatoes for vitamin-rich sweet potatoes. For a wonderful breakfast, serve this dish accompanied by whole-grain toast slathered with strawberry jam.

Sweet Potato Hash

YIELDS 4 HELPIN'S

2 tablespoons nonhydrogenated
   vegan margarine

½ cup chopped onion

3 cups peeled, grated sweet potatoes
   (1 to 1½ pounds)

1 cup frozen veggie burger crumbles,
   thawed, or Ground TSP Beef
   (page 18)

½ cup unsweetened soy milk

1 tablespoon chopped fresh parsley

Salt

Ground pepper

Melt the margarine in a large skillet over medium heat. Add the onion and cook, stirring frequently, for 2 to 3 minutes. Stir in the sweet potatoes and cook without stirring for about 5 minutes. Stir, then let cook undisturbed for 3 minutes longer.

Stir in the veggie burger crumbles and cook, stirring occasionally, until the potatoes are tender, about 5 minutes. Stir in the soy milk and parsley and remove from the heat. Season with salt and pepper to taste.

Per serving: 239 calories, 13 g protein, 6 g fat (2 g sat), 33 g carbs, 360 mg sodium, 70 mg calcium, 5 g fiber

ade from whole wheat pastry flour, antioxidant-rich pecans, omega-3-rich flax-seeds, and cholesterol-lowering cinnamon, these waffles are actually wholesome . . . until you smother 'em in vegan margarine and syrup. But don't let that stop you from dressin' these babies up proper for a tasty breakfast treat. If you don't have a waffle iron, this recipe also works for pancakes (see the variation).

Cinnamon-Pecan Waffles

YIELDS 8 WAFFLES; 4 TO 6 HELPIN'S

½ cup chopped pecans

2 cups plain soy milk

1 tablespoon cider vinegar

¼ cup water

2 tablespoons ground flaxseeds

2 cups whole wheat pastry flour

1 tablespoon ground cinnamon

1 teaspoon baking powder

½ teaspoon baking soda

¼ teaspoon salt

¼ cup canola oil

3 tablespoons maple syrup

1 teaspoon vanilla extract

Toast the pecans in a dry skillet over medium heat, stirring frequently, until lightly browned and fragrant, about 5 minutes.

Spray a waffle iron with cooking spray and heat according to the manufacturer's instructions.

Put the soy milk and vinegar in a small bowl and stir well. Set aside until the soy milk curdles and thickens, about 2 minutes.

Combine the water and flaxseeds in another small bowl and mix well.

Put the flour, cinnamon, baking powder, baking soda, and salt in a large bowl and mix well. Add the soy milk mixture, flaxseed mixture, oil, maple syrup, and vanilla extract and stir until just combined. Don't overmix; a few little lumps are okay. Stir in the pecans.

Spoon about ½ cup of the batter into the waffle iron. You may need more or less batter depending on the size of the waffle iron, but make sure you use enough batter to cover all of the raised squares. Gently close the lid and cook according to the manufacturer's instructions, usually 2 to 4 minutes. Some batter may squish out the sides, and that's okay. Waffle making can be messy.

Repeat with the remaining batter, spraying the waffle iron with more cooking spray after removing each waffle.

CINNAMON-PECAN PANCAKES: Prepare the batter according to the instructions in the main recipe. Spray a large skillet with cooking spray and warm it over medium heat for about 2 minutes. Portion pancakes into the skillet using about ½ cup of batter per pancake and leaving about 2 inches between the pancakes to make it easier to flip them. Cook until the center starts to bubble, the edges have dried out a bit, and the bottom is golden brown, 3 to 4 minutes. Flip and cook until the other side is golden brown, about 3 minutes. You may have to cook the pancakes in several batches.

Per serving (based on 5 servings):
376 calories, 13 g protein, 13 g fat
(1 g sat), 50 g carbs, 223 mg sodium,
116 mg calcium, 8 g fiber

orghum syrup is amazing. Not only is it tantalizingly sweet, it's also loaded with iron and potassium. Who says sweeteners have to be nutritionally bankrupt? As further evidence of its magical powers, with just a little help from baking soda, sorghum syrup morphs into a fluffy topping for pancakes and French toast.

Sorghum-Drizzled French Toast

YIELDS 8 SLICES; 4 HELPIN'S

FRENCH TOAST

1½ cups crumbled extra-firm silken tofu

3 tablespoons maple syrup

1 teaspoon ground cinnamon

1 teaspoon vanilla extract

¼ cup canola oil

8 slices whole-grain bread, toasted

TOPPING

½ cup sorghum syrup

Pinch baking soda

Banana slices or fresh blueberries
(optional)

To make the French toast, put the tofu, maple syrup, cinnamon, and vanilla extract in a food processor. Process until smooth, stopping occasionally to scrape down the work bowl and move the mixture toward the blades. Pour into a shallow bowl that's wide enough to accommodate a slice of the bread.

Line a plate with several layers of paper towels.

Heat the oil in large nonstick skillet over medium heat for 2 to 3 minutes. Put a slice of the toasted bread in the tofu mixture, then turn it over to coat the other side. Put the toast in the skillet and repeat with as many slices as will fit in the skillet without touching. Fry until crisp and golden brown on the bottom, 3 to 4 minutes. Flip and fry until crisp on the other side, about 3 minutes. Transfer to the lined plate to drain. You may have to cook the French toast in several batches.

To top the French toast, put the sorghum syrup in a small saucepan over medium heat. Cook, stirring occasionally, until bubbly. Stir in the baking soda and cook until frothy, less than 1 minute. Remove from the heat and drizzle over the French toast. Top with banana slices or blueberries if desired.

Per serving: 492 calories, 15 g protein, 18 g fat (2 g sat), 71 g carbs, 326 mg sodium, 154 mg calcium, 5 g fiber

hen I was a kid, I loved it when my mom would melt a little cheese in my scrambled eggs. Thankfully, nutritional yeast mixed into scrambled tofu provides a similar cheesy flavor. Feel free to omit the veggies if you like, but they're great for boostin' the nutritional value.

Cheesy Tofu Scramble

YIELDS 4 TO 5 HELPIN'S

3 tablespoons unsweetened soy milk

2 tablespoons nutritional yeast

1 tablespoon reduced-sodium soy sauce

½ teaspoon onion powder

½ teaspoon garlic powder

½ teaspoon ground turmeric

½ teaspoon dried basil

¼ teaspoon celery salt

1 cup finely chopped vegetables (optional; see note)

1 pound extra-firm regular tofu, drained

Put the soy milk, nutritional yeast, soy sauce, onion powder, garlic powder, turmeric, basil, and celery salt in a small bowl and mix well.

Spray a medium skillet with cooking spray. Put the optional vegetables in the skillet and cook over medium heat, stirring frequently, until tender, about 4 minutes. Crumble the tofu into the skillet and stir in the soy milk mixture. Cook, stirring frequently, until the liquid is mostly cooked off, 5 to 7 minutes.

NOTE: I typically toss in whatever veggies I have on hand. Try broccoli, carrots, green onion, mushrooms, red onion, tomatoes—whatever your little heart desires.

Per serving (based on 4.5 servings): 119 calories, 13 g protein, 6 g fat (1 g sat), 4 g carbs, 207 mg sodium, 180 mg calcium, 2 g fiber

orn tortillas, black beans, and South-of-the-border seasoned tofu are an irresistible combination in these breakfast enchiladas. I typically prepare the tofu and bean mixture the evening before so I can quickly put this dish together for breakfast on hectic workdays. Believe it or not, knowing this dish awaits me keeps me from hitting the snooze button on my alarm.

Tofu Scramble Enchiladas

YIELDS 4 TO 6 HELPIN'S

8 ounces extra-firm regular tofu, drained

1½ teaspoons chili powder

½ teaspoon salt

¼ teaspoon garlic powder

¼ teaspoon ground turmeric

1 can (14 to 16 ounces) **black beans,** drained and rinsed

3 to 4 dashes hot sauce

12 corn tortillas

1 cup salsa

Shredded vegan Cheddar cheese (optional)

Preheat the oven to 325 degrees F. Spray a 13 x 9-inch baking pan with cooking spray.

Spray a large skillet with cooking spray. Crumble in the tofu. Add the chili powder, salt, garlic powder, and turmeric and mix well. Cook over medium heat, stirring frequently, until the liquid is mostly cooked off, about 5 minutes. Add the black beans and season with the hot sauce as desired. Cook, stirring frequently, until heated through, about 5 minutes.

Put a small dry skillet over low heat. Put a tortilla in the skillet and cook until lightly browned on the bottom, about 30 seconds. Flip and cook until the other side is lightly browned, 15 to 20 seconds. Transfer to a plate and repeat with the remaining tortillas.

Put 3 tablespoons of the tofu mixture in the center of a tortilla and roll it up, then put it in the prepared pan, seam-side down. Repeat with the remaining tortillas and tofu mixture. Top with the salsa and vegan cheese if desired. Bake for about 10 minutes, until the enchiladas are heated through and the vegan cheese is melted.

NOTE: You can cook the tofu and bean mixture in advance and store it in a sealed container in the refrigerator. In the morning, all you have to do is preheat the oven, heat as many tortillas as desired, then assemble and bake the enchiladas. Save any leftover tofu and bean mixture for the next day.

Per serving (based on 5 servings): 284 calories, 14 g protein, 4 g fat (1 g sat), 41 g carbs, 393 mg sodium, 216 mg calcium, 9 g fiber

Don't let the name fool you. This dish is a far cry from traditional Italian lasagne, laden with tomatoes and cheese. The resemblance lies in the layering technique, used here to assemble several beloved breakfast foods in a casserole dish. This recipe involves multiple steps, so you might want to make it for a special occasion or a leisurely Sunday brunch. If you like, you can prepare the components and layer them in the casserole dish the night before. Just refrigerate the unbaked dish. Then, in the morning, a super-satisfying savory breakfast treat awaits—all you have to do is bake it!

Breakfast Lasagne

YIELDS 6 TO 8 HELPIN'S

1 medium baking potato, peeled and sliced ¼ inch thick

3 tablespoons unsweetened soy milk

1 tablespoon reduced-sodium soy sauce

½ teaspoon onion powder

½ teaspoon garlic powder

½ teaspoon ground turmeric

1 pound extra-firm regular tofu, drained

14 ounces (one tube) Gimme Lean Sausage, sliced into patties

2 cups Basic Cheesy Sauce (page 13)

1 tomato, sliced

Seasoning salt

Salt

Ground pepper

Put the potato in a medium pot and add water to cover. Bring to a boil over high heat. Decrease the heat to medium-low, cover, and cook until fork-tender but not mushy, about 10 minutes. Drain in a colander. Don't worry if a few slices break; they form the bottom layer of the casserole, so it doesn't matter.

Preheat the oven to 350 degrees F. Spray a 4-quart casserole dish with cooking spray.

Put the soy milk, soy sauce, onion powder, garlic powder, and turmeric in a small bowl and mix well.

Spray a large skillet with cooking spray. Crumble in the tofu, then pour in the soy milk mixture. Cook over medium heat, stirring frequently, until the liquid is mostly cooked off, 5 to 7 minutes.

Spray another large skillet with cooking spray. Put the skillet over medium heat, add the vegan sausage, and cook until brown on the bottom, 3 to 4 minutes. Flip the patties and cook until brown on the other side, about 3 minutes. Transfer to a plate and break into bite-sized pieces with a fork.

To assemble the casserole, put the potato slices in the casserole dish in an even layer and sprinkle with seasoning salt. Spread the vegan sausage over the potato in an even layer. Spread the tofu over the vegan sausage in an even layer. Pour the cheesy sauce evenly over the top. Arrange the tomato slices evenly over the sauce and season with salt and pepper.

Bake uncovered for 25 minutes, until heated through.

Per serving (based on 7 servings): 237 calories, 21 g protein, 7 g fat (1 g sat), 22 g carbs, 556 mg sodium, 169 mg calcium, 7 g fiber

For years, Southern cooks have been saving their meat drippings to flavor redeye gravy. This thin sauce is typically made with a mixture of ham grease and strong black coffee, but my vegan version draws its pork-like flavor from the seasonings in the tofu marinade, thank goodness. For a classic Southern breakfast, pour the gravy over the tofu ham and sop up any extra gravy with Whole Wheat Buttermilk Biscuits (page 136).

Brown Sugar—Baked Tofu Ham with Redeye Gravy

Advance preparation required   **YIELDS 8 SLICES; 4 TO 6 HELPIN'S**

TOFU HAM

1 pound extra-firm regular tofu, drained and pressed (see page 5)

2 cups low-sodium vegetable broth

¼ cup reduced-sodium soy sauce

2 tablespoons nutritional yeast

1 tablespoon brown sugar

1 teaspoon onion powder

GRAVY

1 cup strong black coffee

6 tablespoons reserved marinade from the Tofu Ham

1 tablespoon extra-virgin olive oil

Salt

To make the tofu ham, slice the tofu into 8 equal slabs.

Put the broth, soy sauce, nutritional yeast, brown sugar, and onion powder in a large, shallow storage container. Whisk until thoroughly blended.

Put the tofu in the container and gently flip the slabs over to evenly coat them with the marinade. Cover and refrigerate for 8 to 12 hours, turning the tofu once or twice during the marinating time.

Preheat the oven to 425 degrees F. Spray a baking sheet with cooking spray or line it with parchment paper.

Remove the tofu from the marinade and reserve 6 tablespoons of the marinade; discard the rest. Put the tofu on the prepared baking sheet and bake for 25 minutes, until lightly browned, carefully flipping the tofu halfway through the baking time.

To make the gravy, put the coffee, reserved marinade, and oil in a small saucepan and mix well. Cook over medium heat for 5 minutes. Season with salt to taste. Spoon the gravy liberally over the tofu ham.

Per serving (based on 5 servings): 134 calories, 12 g protein, 8 g fat (1 g sat), 5 g carbs, 237 mg sodium, 165 mg calcium, 1 g fiber

outherners eat fried chicken for every meal, including breakfast. So why shouldn't vegans enjoy fried tofu for every meal? This is a simple breakfast sandwich that uses two recipes included in other chapters of the book. This dish might be a little too labor-intensive and indulgent for a weekday breakfast, but it's ideal for a sinful weekend brunch. It's also perfect for using up leftover Southern Fried Tofu Chicken.

Southern Tofu Chicken Biscuits

Advance preparation required   **YIELDS 4 HELPIN'S**

4 Whole Wheat Buttermilk Biscuits (page 136)**, freshly baked and kept warm**

Dijon mustard

4 slices Southern Fried Tofu Chicken (page 90)**, freshly fried and kept warm**

Slice the biscuits open and spread mustard evenly over the inside surfaces. Put a slice of Tofu Chicken on the bottom half of each biscuit and top with the remaining halves of the biscuits.

Per serving (with large biscuits): 449 calories, 18 g protein, 20 g fat (3 g sat), 46 g carbs, 755 mg sodium, 253 mg calcium, 9 g fiber

Per serving (with small biscuits): 342 calories, 14 g protein, 15 g fat (2 g sat), 34 g carbs, 525 mg sodium, 178 mg calcium, 6 g fiber

DON'T SPOIL YOUR SUPPER

APPETIZERS AND SNACKS

If there's one thing to be said about Southern folks, it's that we know how to throw a great party. From family reunions and church potlucks to college keggers and bad-ass birthday throwdowns, we know the food is what makes or breaks a festive occasion. Fancy hors d'oeuvres are fine for a stuffy gathering, but the easy appetizers in this section are more fitting for a fun get-together with close friends and family who are less impressed with gourmet showmanship and more appreciative of down-home eats with great taste.

Offer up a platter of Butter Bean Bruschetta (page 39) or Deviled Tofu Bites (page 42) at your next soiree. Try the Cajun Boiled Peanuts (page 38) for a true Dirty South snack, or nosh on a Cheesy Un-chicken Quesadilla (page 44) before diggin' in to your main course. But don't pig out too much, or you'll spoil your supper.

The versatile chickpea makes for great hummus, but substituting black-eyed peas lends this Mediterranean spread some Southern flair. Serve it with toasted pita chips or raw veggies.

Garlicky Black-Eyed Pea Hummus

MAKES 1¼ CUPS; 10 HELPIN'S

1 can (14 to 16 ounces) **black-eyed peas, drained and rinsed**

¼ **cup tahini**

3 **tablespoons extra-virgin olive oil**

1 **tablespoon freshly squeezed lemon juice**

2 **cloves garlic, minced**

½ **teaspoon salt**

¼ **to** ½ **cup water**

Paprika, for garnish

Put the black-eyed peas, tahini, 2 tablespoons of the oil, and the lemon juice, garlic, and salt in a food processor. Process until combined but still a bit chunky, stopping occasionally to scrape down the work bowl and move the mixture toward the blades.

With the processor running, slowly drizzle in about ¼ cup of the water. Process until smooth and creamy. If storing the hummus in the refrigerator for several hours before serving, drizzle in the remaining water and process until smooth, as the hummus tends to thicken as it sits.

To serve, transfer to a serving bowl and drizzle the remaining tablespoon of oil over the top. Lightly dust with paprika.

Per 2 tablespoons: 87 calories, 2 g protein, 7 g fat (1 g sat), 3 g carbs, 112 mg sodium, 48 mg calcium, 1 g fiber

For every Southern church potluck and family reunion, you can bet your bottom dollar that somebody brought a big ol' pot of Ro*Tel cheese dip, a melty mixture of processed cheese and canned diced tomatoes with green chiles. Though it doesn't sound like a dairy product, processed cheese is indeed made from cheese. But never fear: this creamy nondairy dip will fool all the blue-haired ladies at the next church potluck. They'll never know it's dairy-free unless you tell 'em. Serve this dip with tortilla chips.

No-Tell Ro*Tel Cheese Dip

MAKES 2 CUPS; 8 HELPIN'S

1½ cups crumbled extra-firm silken tofu

¾ cup nutritional yeast

1 cup canned diced tomatoes with green chiles, with juice

1 tablespoon extra-virgin olive oil

½ teaspoon salt

½ teaspoon ground turmeric

¼ teaspoon garlic powder

¼ teaspoon onion powder

Put the tofu, nutritional yeast, ½ cup of the tomatoes with green chiles with their juice, and the oil, salt, turmeric, garlic powder, and onion powder in a food processor. Process until smooth, stopping occasionally to scrape down the work bowl and move the mixture toward the blades.

Transfer the mixture to a small saucepan and stir in the remaining tomatoes with green chiles with their juice. Cook over low heat, stirring occasionally, until hot and bubbly, 5 to 7 minutes. Serve immediately.

Per ¼ cup: 70 calories, 7 g protein, 3 g fat (0 g sat), 4 g carbs, 289 mg sodium, 27 mg calcium, 2 g fiber

I know "boiled peanuts" probably doesn't sound appetizing, but just trust me on this one. My dad and I discovered this Southern delicacy on a road trip down the historic Natchez Trace Parkway in Mississippi. We stopped at a small mom-and-pop gas station that sold Cajun-spiced boiled peanuts in the shell, and even though we were skeptical at first, we were instant converts after one taste. Boiling magically transforms ordinarily crunchy peanuts, giving them the appearance, flavor, and texture of slow-cooked Cajun-spiced beans. To enjoy them, just remove the tough shell and enjoy the salty, soft peanuts inside.

Cajun Boiled Peanuts

MAKES ABOUT 9 CUPS; 18 HELPIN'S

20 ounces roasted unshelled peanuts

3 tablespoons seafood boil seasoning
(see note)

1½ teaspoons salt

Sort through the peanuts and discard any debris. Put the unshelled peanuts in a colander and rinse well.

Put the peanuts, seafood boil seasoning, and salt in a slow cooker and add water to cover. Cover and cook on the high setting for 12 hours, adding water as needed to keep the peanuts covered. After the peanuts are cooked, they can be kept warm in the cooker on the low setting for up to 2 hours.

NOTE: Seafood boil seasoning is a dry mixture of whole and crumbled or ground spices. It can be found in the seafood section and sometimes the spice aisle of most grocery stores.

NOTE: I recommend serving the peanuts right away, while they're still warm, but any leftovers will keep for about a week in the fridge.

Per ½ cup: 125 calories, 6 g protein, 9 g fat (2 g sat), 5 g carbs, 102 mg sodium, 15 mg calcium, 1 g fiber

outhern cuisine meets fancy Italian fare in this twist on the classic tomato-topped crostini. Butter beans, a pale version of lima beans, are as ubiquitous as kudzu and sweet tea in the South. In this recipe, toasted baguette slices are topped with a garlicky butter bean spread, juicy tomatoes, fresh basil, and creamy avocado. Serve it at all your fancy gatherin's.

Butter Bean Bruschetta

MAKES 16 TO 20 HELPIN'S

BRUSCHETTA

1 baguette

1 large tomato, chopped

1 ripe but firm avocado, diced

¼ cup minced red onion

2 tablespoons chopped fresh basil

1 tablespoon extra-virgin olive oil

1 tablespoon freshly squeezed lemon juice

½ teaspoon salt

Ground pepper

BUTTER BEAN SPREAD

1 can (14 to 16 ounces) **butter beans, drained and rinsed**

1 tablespoon extra-virgin olive oil

1 clove garlic, minced

¼ teaspoon salt

⅛ teaspoon ground pepper

1 to 2 tablespoons water

To make the bruschetta, preheat the oven to 350 degrees F.

Slice the baguette diagonally into 16 to 20 slices, each about 1 inch thick. Put the slices on a baking sheet and bake for 7 to 10 minutes, until lightly browned and toasted to your liking.

Put the tomato, avocado, onion, basil, oil, lemon juice, and salt in a large bowl and mix well. Season with pepper to taste.

To make the spread, put the beans, oil, garlic, salt, and pepper in a food processor. Process until creamy, stopping occasionally to scrape down the work bowl and move the mixture toward the blades. With the processor running, add 1 to 2 tablespoons of water as needed to achieve the desired consistency. Process again until very creamy.

To assemble, spread a rounded tablespoonful of the bean spread over each baguette slice. Scoop out 2 tablespoons of the tomato mixture using a slotted spoon and put it atop the bean spread. Serve immediately.

Per serving (based on 18 servings): 118 calories, 4 g protein, 4 g fat (1 g sat), 15 g carbs, 201 mg sodium, 27 mg calcium, 2 g fiber

Okay, so these are really just plain ol' fritters. But since they're dressed up with a creamy roasted red bell pepper sauce, it sounds fancier to call 'em corn cakes. Serve these to whet your guests' appetites at a special dinner party, or serve them as the main course at a less elaborate gatherin'.

Black-Eyed Pea Corn Cakes with Roasted Red Bell Pepper Sauce

MAKES 8 CORN CAKES; 4 TO 8 HELPIN'S

ROASTED RED BELL PEPPER SAUCE

1 cup crumbled firm silken tofu

1 cup chopped roasted red bell peppers, patted dry with paper towels

2 tablespoons freshly squeezed lemon juice

½ teaspoon onion powder

¼ teaspoon salt

¼ teaspoon ground cumin

CORN CAKES

1 cup whole wheat pastry flour

1 teaspoon baking powder

½ teaspoon salt, plus more for sprinkling if desired

¼ teaspoon garlic powder

2 tablespoons water

1 tablespoon ground flaxseeds

¾ cup unsweetened soy milk

1 cup frozen corn kernels, thawed, plus more for garnish

1 cup canned black-eyed peas, drained and rinsed, plus more for garnish

¼ cup canola oil, plus more if needed

To make the sauce, put all the ingredients in a food processor. Process until smooth, stopping occasionally to scrape down the work bowl and move the mixture toward the blades.

To make the corn cakes, put the flour, baking powder, salt, and garlic powder in a large bowl and mix well.

Put the water and flaxseeds in a small bowl and mix well. Add the soy milk and whisk until thoroughly blended. Pour into the flour mixture and stir until just combined. Gently stir in the corn and black-eyed peas.

Line a plate with several layers of paper towels.

Heat the oil in a large, heavy skillet over medium heat. The oil should generously coat the bottom of the skillet; if it doesn't, add more oil as needed, 1 tablespoon at a time. Sprinkle a pinch of flour over the oil to check the heat. If the oil sizzles, it's ready.

Scoop out ¼ cup of the corn cake batter and carefully pour it into the skillet. Repeat until the skillet is full but not overcrowded; the corn cakes shouldn't touch. You may have to cook them in batches.

Fry until brown on the bottom, 2 to 3 minutes. Flip the cakes and fry until the other side is brown, about 2 minutes. Transfer to the lined plate to drain.

To serve, sprinkle the cakes with additional salt if desired. Top each with 1 to 2 tablespoons of the sauce. Garnish with additional corn and black-eyed peas. Serve warm.

Per serving (based on 6 servings): 262 calories, 9 g protein, 12 g fat (1 g sat), 26 g carbs, 361 mg sodium, 126 mg calcium, 6 g fiber

Typically, sausage balls are made with pork sausage, Cheddar cheese, and biscuit mix—definitely not vegan! This version relies instead on meatless sausage, sweet potatoes, and flour. Guests at your next soiree won't even miss the meat when you serve these on a platter with a bowl of cheesy, spicy dipping sauce.

Sweet Potato–Sausage Balls with Cheesy Chili Dipping Sauce

MAKES ABOUT 30 BALLS; 10 HELPIN'S

2 large sweet potatoes, peeled and cubed

1¾ cups whole wheat pastry flour, plus more for kneading

3 tablespoons nutritional yeast

1 teaspoon baking powder

1 teaspoon salt

½ teaspoon baking soda

7 ounces (one-half tube) **Gimme Lean Sausage**

¼ cup water

2 tablespoons canola oil

1½ cups Spicy Cheesy Sauce (page 13), **kept warm**

Put the sweet potatoes in a large pot and add water to cover. Bring to a boil over high heat. Decrease the heat to medium-low, cover, and cook until fork-tender, about 20 minutes. Drain, then rinse under cold water until cool enough to handle. You'll be digging your hands in soon, and you don't want to burn your fingers.

Preheat the oven to 350 degrees F. Line a large baking sheet with parchment paper.

Put 1 cup of the flour and the nutritional yeast, baking powder, salt, and baking soda in a medium bowl and mix well.

Put the sweet potatoes in a large bowl and mash with a potato masher or a fork. Measure out 2 cups of the sweet potatoes (reserve any leftovers for another use) and put them back in the bowl. Add the vegan sausage and knead it into the potatoes using your hands. Add the water and canola oil and stir or use your hands to combine. Add the flour mixture and knead until thoroughly combined. Add the remaining ¾ cup of flour and knead until just incorporated.

Coat your hands with flour. Scoop out about 2 tablespoons of the mixture and roll it into a ball between the palms of your hands. Put it on the lined baking sheet. Repeat with the remaining sweet potato mixture to make about 30 sausage balls. Bake for 15 minutes, then turn the balls over and bake for 15 minutes longer, until firm and golden brown.

Arrange the sausage balls on a platter. Pour the warm cheesy sauce into a bowl and serve alongside the sausage balls.

Per 3 balls with sauce: 248 calories, 10 g protein, 5 g fat (1 g sat), 39 g carbs, 554 mg sodium, 95 mg calcium, 8 g fiber

A t special events and Thanksgiving feasts with my family, the deviled eggs rarely made it to the dinner table. That's because no one could keep from sneaking one or two from the milk-glass retro egg plate in the fridge. I was among the guilty, and now that I've developed these vegan deviled tofu bites, I can continue the tradition of stuffing my face before dinner. Black salt is the magical ingredient in these babies, so don't make 'em without it.

Deviled Tofu Bites

MAKES 24 PIECES; 12 HELPIN'S

1 pound extra-firm regular tofu, drained and pressed (see page 5)

1 cup crumbled firm silken tofu

1 cup canned Great Northern beans, drained and rinsed

2 tablespoons vegan mayonnaise or Tofu Mayo (page 8)

3½ teaspoons black salt (see page 1)

1 tablespoon yellow mustard

1 teaspoon ground turmeric

1 tablespoon dill pickle relish, drained

1½ teaspoons minced red onion

Ground pepper

Paprika, for garnish

Chopped fresh chives, for garnish

Cut the block of pressed regular tofu into quarters, then cut each quarter into 6 equal pieces, to make 24 pieces in all.

Put the silken tofu, beans, vegan mayonnaise, ½ teaspoon of the black salt, and the mustard and turmeric in a food processor. Process until smooth, stopping occasionally to scrape down the work bowl and move the mixture toward the blades. Transfer to a medium bowl and stir in the pickle relish and onion. Season with pepper to taste.

Put the remaining 3 teaspoons of black salt in a small bowl. Using your fingertip, rub a touch of the black salt over each piece of the pressed tofu. (You may have extra black salt left after spreading.) Put a dollop (about 1 teaspoon) of the silken tofu mixture on top (reserve any leftover topping to spread on toast or crackers). Garnish with paprika and chives.

Per serving: 79 calories, 8 g protein, 3 g fat (0 g sat), 4 g carbs, 356 mg sodium, 85 mg calcium, 2 g fiber

Sweet-and-sour meatballs lurking under the lid of a slow cooker are a common item on buffet tables in the South. I don't think it's an exclusively Southern recipe, but it's definitely redneck fare at its finest—and we've got plenty of that in the South! Serve these bean-based meatballs at your next trailer park potluck, and you'll be the envy of all of your big-haired neighbors in daisy dukes. (That's slang for really short cutoff shorts, in case y'all didn't know.)

Sweet 'n' Sour Bean Balls

MAKES ABOUT 20 BALLS; 10 HELPIN'S

BEAN BALLS

½ cup dry **TSP crumbles** (see page 5)

¾ cup **boiling water**

1 can (14 to 16 ounces) **pinto beans, drained and rinsed**

2 tablespoons **vegan Worcestershire sauce** (homemade, page 10, or store-bought)

1 tablespoon **reduced-sodium soy sauce**

½ teaspoon **onion powder**

½ cup dry **whole wheat breadcrumbs**

2 tablespoons **vital wheat gluten**

SWEET 'N' SOUR SAUCE

1 cup **ketchup**

¼ cup **water**

1½ tablespoons **cider vinegar**

½ teaspoon **chili powder**

½ teaspoon **onion powder**

¼ teaspoon **salt**

¼ teaspoon **garlic powder**

½ cup **grape jelly**

To make the bean balls, preheat the oven to 400 degrees F. Line a baking sheet with parchment paper.

Put the TSP in a small heatproof bowl. Add the boiling water and let sit for 5 minutes to rehydrate. Drain in a fine-mesh sieve.

Put the beans in a medium bowl and mash with a potato masher or a fork until fairly smooth. Stir in the Worcestershire sauce, soy sauce, and onion powder. Add the TSP and mix well. Add the breadcrumbs and vital wheat gluten and use your hands to mix and knead until thoroughly combined.

Scoop out 1 tablespoon of the bean mixture and roll it into a ball between the palms of your hands. Put it on the lined baking sheet. Repeat with the remaining bean mixture to make about 20 balls. Bake for 10 minutes, then turn the balls over and bake for 10 to 15 minutes longer, until golden brown.

To make the sauce, put the ketchup, water, vinegar, chili powder, onion powder, salt, and garlic powder in a small saucepan and mix well. Add the jelly and stir it in as well as possible. Cook over medium-low heat, stirring occasionally, until the jelly melts and is evenly incorporated, 5 to 10 minutes. Remove from the heat.

To serve, put the baked bean balls in the sauce, 3 or 4 at a time, and gently stir to coat. Remove with a slotted spoon and transfer to a serving platter or bowl. Repeat until all the bean balls are coated with sauce. Pour any remaining sauce over the bean balls just before serving. Serve hot.

Per 2 balls: 123 calories, 6 g protein, 0 g fat (0 g sat), 23 g carbs, 532 mg sodium, 35 mg calcium, 2 g fiber

These quesadillas are stuffed with seitan and a creamy mixture of nutritional yeast and shredded vegan cheese. Cut 'em up into small wedges to serve at a party, or make a meal for two out of the whole quesadillas.

Cheesy Un-chicken Quesadillas

MAKES 2 QUESADILLAS; 2 TO 8 HELPIN'S

2 teaspoons extra-virgin olive oil

2 cloves garlic, minced

8 button mushrooms, sliced

1 cup thinly sliced seitan or Seitan Chicken (page 16)

½ cup water

¼ cup nutritional yeast

1 tablespoon reduced-sodium soy sauce

2 teaspoons chili powder

2 (8-inch) flour tortillas

½ cup shredded vegan Cheddar cheese

Salsa, for serving (optional)

Vegan sour cream, for serving (optional)

Heat the oil in a medium skillet over medium heat. Add the garlic and cook, stirring constantly, for 1 minute. Add the mushrooms and seitan and cook, stirring frequently, until the mushrooms begin to cook down, 5 to 7 minutes.

Add the water, nutritional yeast, soy sauce, and chili powder and mix well. Increase the heat to medium-high heat and cook, stirring frequently, until the liquid is absorbed, about 8 minutes.

Spray a large skillet with cooking spray and put it over medium heat. Put 1 tortilla in the skillet. Put half of the seitan mixture on one side of the tortilla and top with ¼ cup of the vegan cheese.

Fold the tortilla over the mixture and cook until the bottom is lightly browned, 1 to 2 minutes. Carefully flip and cook until the other side is lightly browned, about 1 minute.

Transfer the quesadilla to a plate and repeat with the second tortilla and the remaining seitan mixture and cheese. Slice each quesadilla into 2 to 4 wedges. Serve with salsa and vegan sour cream if desired.

Per serving (based on 8 servings): 102 calories, 9 g protein, 3 g fat (1 g sat), 10 g carbs, 280 mg sodium, 31 mg calcium, 2 g fiber

No piggies were harmed in the making of these party snacks. After all, shouldn't a treat called pigs in a blanket be pig-friendly?

Save-the-Pigs in a Blanket

MAKES 24 PIECES; 12 HELPIN'S

- 8 veggie dogs
- 2 cups whole wheat pastry flour, plus more for sprinkling
- 1 teaspoon baking powder
- ¼ teaspoon salt
- ¼ teaspoon baking soda
- ¾ cup ice water

Preheat the oven to 425 degrees F. Line a baking sheet with parchment paper.

Cut each veggie dog crosswise into 3 equal pieces, for a total of 24 pieces.

Put the flour, baking powder, salt, and baking soda in a large bowl and mix well. Pour in the ice water and stir until a dough forms. Shape the dough into a ball.

Sprinkle a little flour on a sheet of waxed paper (see note) or a clean work surface and put the dough on the floured surface. Sprinkle a few pinches of flour over the dough, then flatten the dough with your hands, shaping it into a square. Use a rolling pin to roll the dough out to an 11 x 9-inch rectangle with a short end facing you.

Use a knife to cut the dough into 6 equal lengthwise strips, using a piece of veggie dog as a reference for the size needed. The strips should be slightly narrower than the length of the veggie dog pieces. (When you roll them, you'll want a little bit of veggie dog sticking out on both ends.)

Put a piece of veggie dog crosswise at the bottom of one long strip and roll it up in the dough until it's just covered all the way around. Cut the dough from the strip at that point and press the ends of the dough "blanket" together with your fingers. Put the rolled veggie dog on the lined baking sheet. Repeat until all the veggie dog pieces are wrapped.

Bake for 13 to 15 minutes, until the dough is golden brown.

NOTE: If you use waxed paper to roll out the dough, sprinkle a little water on the countertop first to keep the waxed paper from sliding.

Per 2 pieces: 106 calories, 9 g protein, 1 g fat (0 g sat), 15 g carbs, 267 mg sodium, 48 mg calcium, 3 g fiber

LADIES (AND GENTLEMEN) WHO LUNCH

SALADS AND SANDWICHES

Fresh green salads are a staple in almost every food culture, but who needs a recipe for combining greens and raw vegetables? The salads in this chapter are mostly on the more substantial side, such as Dill Weed Potato Salad (page 54) and Eggless Tofu-Olive Salad (page 55). But you will find recipes for a few lettuce-based salads, like Seitan and Red Pear Salad (page 56) and White-Trash Pineapple Salad (page 51; don't knock it 'til you've tried it, y'all).

Although these satisfying salads can stand on their own, they also make excellent sides to the sandwiches in this chapter. These hearty sandwich recipes are perfect for a weekday lunch or light supper. Try Fried Green Tomato and Tofu Sandwiches (page 63) or Fried Tofu Chicken Wafflewiches with Maple-Mustard Sauce (page 64) for a true Southern treat.

othing refreshes like ice-cold watermelon on a scorching-hot day. In this recipe it's jazzed up with spicy jalapeño chile, tangy lime juice, and sweet basil.

Jalapeño-Lime Watermelon Salad

See photo facing page 23.

MAKES 4 HELPIN'S

3 cups chilled, cubed watermelon

1 tablespoon minced jalapeño chile

1 tablespoon chopped fresh basil

Juice of 1 lime

Salt

Put the watermelon, chile, and basil in a medium bowl. Sprinkle the lime juice over the top and stir gently to combine. Season with salt to taste. Serve immediately or refrigerate until ready to serve.

Per serving: 38 calories, 1 g protein, 0 g fat (0 g sat), 9 g carbs, 1 mg sodium, 10 mg calcium, 1 g fiber

his is what summer should taste like. Ripe, juicy tomatoes, crunchy green bell pepper, and sweet Vidalia onion combine with a tangy marinade for the perfect warm-weather salad. Warning: Don't make this dish with tasteless winter tomatoes. It will be subpar, and you'll regret it.

Summer Tomato Salad

Advance preparation required

2 large tomatoes, cut into large chunks

1 green bell pepper, cut into large pieces

1 large cucumber, peeled and sliced

½ Vidalia onion or red onion, diced

2 tablespoons rice vinegar

2 tablespoons extra-virgin olive oil

1½ tablespoons sugar

½ teaspoon salt

Pinch ground pepper

Put the tomatoes, bell pepper, cucumber, and onion in a large bowl and stir gently to combine.

Put the vinegar, oil, sugar, salt, and pepper in a small bowl. Whisk briskly until thoroughly blended. Pour over the vegetables and stir gently until the vegetables are evenly coated. Refrigerate for at least 1 hour before serving to allow the flavors to meld. Stir again before serving.

Per serving (based on 5 servings): 103 calories, 1 g protein, 6 g fat (1 g sat), 10 g carbs, 219 mg sodium, 24 mg calcium, 2 g fiber

y granny serves this colorful salad at large family meals, but it also doubles as a unique tomato-free salsa for dippin' corn chips.

Southwestern Corn Salad

MAKES 6 HELPIN'S

3½ cups frozen corn kernels, thawed

½ cup diced red bell pepper

½ cup diced green bell pepper

¼ cup diced Vidalia onion

¼ cup chopped green onion

10 to 12 black olives, sliced

2 tablespoons balsamic vinegar

2 tablespoons extra-virgin olive oil

1 tablespoon cider vinegar

1 tablespoon sugar

¼ teaspoon celery salt

⅛ teaspoon ground cumin

⅛ teaspoon paprika

⅛ teaspoon cayenne, plus more
   if desired

Salt

Ground pepper

Put the corn, red bell pepper, green bell pepper, Vidalia onion, green onion, and olives in a large bowl and mix well.

Put the balsamic vinegar, oil, cider vinegar, sugar, celery salt, cumin, paprika, and cayenne in a small bowl and whisk briskly until thoroughly blended. Pour over the vegetables and stir until the vegetables are evenly coated. Season with salt, pepper, and more cayenne to taste if desired. Refrigerate until ready to serve.

Per serving: 159 calories, 3 g protein, 6 g fat (1 g sat), 23 g carbs, 140 mg sodium, 19 mg calcium, 4 g fiber

Okay, so maybe pineapple isn't all that Southern, but my dad grew up eating this retro tropical salad in rural Arkansas. Apparently, pineapple salads were popular with the blue-collar Southern folks back in his day. He uses mayo, iceberg lettuce, Cheddar cheese, and pineapple, so with just a couple of substitutions, the recipe is easily veganized.

White-Trash Pineapple Salad

See photo facing page 55.

MAKES 2 HELPIN'S

4 cups chopped romaine lettuce

⅔ cup vegan mayonnaise or Tofu Mayo (page 8)

6 pineapple rings

½ cup shredded vegan Cheddar cheese

Divide the lettuce between two plates. Top each plate with ⅓ cup of the vegan mayonnaise. Arrange 3 pineapple rings over the mayo on each plate, then sprinkle ¼ cup of the vegan cheese over each salad. Serve immediately.

NOTE: You can substitute chopped pineapple, but the intact rings make for a fancier presentation—the key to successful white-trash cookin'!

Per serving: 318 calories, 15 g protein, 16 g fat (2 g sat), 30 g carbs, 453 mg sodium, 67 mg calcium, 5 g fiber

 o respectable barbecue sandwich is served without coleslaw, and this light salad is perfect atop my BBQ "Pulled" Tempeh and Carrot Sandwiches (page 65). It's also mighty fine enjoyed solo or as a side dish for any Southern meal.

Creamy Poppy Seed Coleslaw

See photo facing page 86.

MAKES 4 TO 6 HELPIN'S

3 cups shredded cabbage

1 carrot, peeled and grated

2 tablespoons minced red onion

½ cup vegan mayonnaise or Tofu Mayo (page 8)

1 teaspoon agave nectar

½ teaspoon salt

½ teaspoon poppy seeds

Put the cabbage, carrot, and onion in a large bowl and mix well. Add the vegan mayonnaise, agave nectar, salt, and poppy seeds and stir until the vegetables are evenly coated. Refrigerate until ready to serve.

Per serving (based on 5 servings): 65 calories, 3 g protein, 3 g fat (0 g sat), 5 g carbs, 493 mg sodium, 35 mg calcium, 2 g fiber

This cool and crisp broccoli salad packs a doubly spicy punch, thanks to crushed red pepper flakes and sriracha sauce. If you can't find sriracha sauce, substitute your favorite hot sauce instead. If you can't handle the heat, get out of the kitchen . . . or just omit one (or both) of the spicy ingredients.

Broccoli Salad with Spicy Citrus Vinaigrette

MAKES 4 TO 6 HELPIN'S

1 large head broccoli

1 teaspoon grated lemon zest

1 tablespoon freshly squeezed lemon juice

1 tablespoon cider vinegar

1 tablespoon extra-virgin olive oil

1½ teaspoons agave nectar

1 to 3 teaspoons sriracha sauce

1 teaspoon crushed red pepper flakes

Salt

Ground pepper

Cut the stems off the broccoli and trim away the tough end. Peel the stems with a vegetable peeler, then chop them into bite-sized pieces. Cut the broccoli tops into bite-sized florets. Steam the broccoli florets and stems until just tender, about 4 minutes. Rinse under cold water to stop the cooking, then transfer to a large bowl.

Put the lemon zest, lemon juice, vinegar, oil, agave nectar, 1 teaspoon of the sriracha sauce, and the red pepper flakes in a small bowl and whisk briskly until thoroughly blended. Pour over the broccoli and stir until the broccoli is evenly coated. Season with salt, pepper, and more sriracha sauce to taste if desired. Refrigerate for at least 30 minutes before serving to allow the flavors to meld.

Per serving (based on 5 servings): 57 calories, 2 g protein, 3 g fat (0 g sat), 5 g carbs, 53 mg sodium, 34 mg calcium, 2 g fiber

Dill is one damn tasty herb. In fact, it's one of my favorites. The combination of dill weed and vegan mayonnaise in this down-home potato salad makes it a surefire winner for your next barbecue or picnic.

Dill Weed Potato Salad

16 to 18 small red new potatoes,
scrubbed and quartered

¾ cup vegan mayonnaise or Tofu
Mayo (page 8)

1 stalk celery, diced

10 pimiento-stuffed green olives or
pitted green olives, sliced

2 tablespoons minced onion

1 tablespoon red wine vinegar

2 teaspoons Dijon mustard

2 teaspoons dried dill weed

1 teaspoon chopped fresh chives

1 teaspoon minced jalapeño chile

Salt

Ground pepper

Put the potatoes in a large pot and add water to cover. Bring to a boil over high heat. Decrease the heat to medium-low, cover, and cook until fork-tender, about 20 minutes. Drain, then rinse under cold water to stop the cooking. Let cool completely.

Put the potatoes in a large bowl. Add the vegan mayonnaise, celery, olives, onion, vinegar, mustard, dill weed, chives, and chile and stir until thoroughly combined. Season with salt and pepper to taste. Refrigerate until ready to serve.

Per serving (based on 5 servings): 492 calories, 13 g protein, 6 g fat (1 g sat), 99 g carbs, 319 mg sodium, 71 mg calcium, 9 g fiber

Fried Green Tomato and Tofu Sandwich, *page 63*

Roasted Veggie Po'Boy, *page 58,* **with White-Trash Pineapple Salad,** *page 51*

y mama always puts green olives in her egg salad, which really steps it up a few notches. Subbing crumbled tofu for eggs steps up this salad even more. Serve it atop crisp romaine lettuce, or put it on whole-grain bread for a satisfying sandwich.

Eggless Tofu-Olive Salad

MAKES 2 CUPS; 4 HELPIN'S

1 pound extra-firm regular tofu, drained and pressed (see page 5)

½ cup vegan mayonnaise or Tofu Mayo (page 8)

¼ cup minced celery

¼ cup sliced pimiento-stuffed green olives or pitted green olives

2 tablespoons minced red onion

1 tablespoon nutritional yeast

1 teaspoon dried parsley

½ teaspoon ground turmeric

½ teaspoon black salt (see page 1), **or ¼ teaspoon regular salt**

Ground pepper

Crumble the tofu into a medium bowl. Add the vegan mayonnaise, celery, olives, onion, nutritional yeast, parsley, turmeric, and black salt and stir until thoroughly combined. Season with pepper to taste. Refrigerate until ready to serve.

Per ½ cup: 189 calories, 17 g protein, 11 g fat (1 g sat), 6 g carbs, 385 mg sodium, 223 mg calcium, 2 g fiber

I've always been a throw-every-veggie-in-the-fridge-into-my-salad kind of gal. But sometimes using only a few carefully selected ingredients results in something especially delicious.

Seitan and Red Pear Salad

MAKES 2 HELPIN'S

2 cups mixed baby greens, lightly packed

1 red pear with peel, cubed

½ cup sliced cold seitan or Seitan Chicken (page 16)

2 tablespoons chopped raw walnuts

1 green onion, sliced

1 tablespoon extra-virgin olive oil

1 tablespoon pear-infused white balsamic vinegar or regular white balsamic vinegar

1 clove garlic, minced

Pinch salt

Pinch ground pepper

Put the greens, pear, seitan, walnuts, and green onion in a large bowl and toss gently to combine.

Put the oil, vinegar, garlic, salt, and pepper in a small jar with a lid. Screw on the lid and shake well to combine. Pour over the salad and toss gently until the greens are evenly coated. Serve immediately.

Per serving: 233 calories, 12 g protein, 12 g fat (1 g sat), 18 g carbs, 207 mg sodium, 68 mg calcium, 4 g fiber

When I was a kid, my parents occasionally treated me to a gigantic barbecued pulled pork salad from a little country gas station called Big Al's. I know what you're thinking: Barbecue from a gas station?! Yes, indeed. I remember that salad of tangy barbecue, shredded cheese, and ranch dressing being quite delicious. However, I wasn't too fond of lettuce back then, so I'd order my salad with, um, no salad. Just meat, cheese, and dressing. These days, my salads are far more nutritious. This veganized version of the Big Al's salad substitutes seitan for pulled pork and has a lot more veggies.

BBQ Seitan Salad

MAKES 2 HELPIN'S

1 cup sliced seitan or Seitan Chicken (page 16)

6 tablespoons barbecue sauce (homemade, page 12, or store-bought)

2 cups chopped romaine hearts

1 large tomato, diced

¾ cup diced red bell pepper

¾ cup peeled and diced cucumber

6 radishes, sliced

3 tablespoons sliced green onion

Salt

Ground pepper

3 tablespoons vegan bacon bits

Shredded vegan Cheddar cheese (optional)

Vegan ranch dressing or Country Buttermilk Ranch Dressing (page 9)

Put the seitan and barbecue sauce in a small saucepan and stir until the seitan is evenly coated. Cook over medium-low heat, stirring frequently, until the seitan and sauce are warmed through, about 10 minutes. Let cool.

Layer the lettuce, tomato, bell pepper, cucumber, radishes, and green onion on two large plates. Season with salt and pepper as desired. Top each salad with half of the seitan and bacon bits and as much vegan cheese and ranch dressing as desired. Serve immediately.

Per serving: 309 calories, 26 g protein, 7 g fat (3 g sat), 35 g carbs, 890 mg sodium, 167 mg calcium, 7 g fiber

A po'boy (slang for "poor boy") is a submarine sandwich served on a baguette. Down in Louisiana, they use a special kind of bread with a soft, airy center and typically fill it with something fishy and fried, like oysters or crawfish. This vegan version is piled high with roasted veggies. If you can get your hands on fancy Louisiana baguettes, more power to ya. But feel free to use regular supermarket baguettes instead.

Roasted Veggie Po'Boys

See photo facing page 55.

MAKES 4 HELPIN'S

1 medium summer squash, cut in half crosswise, then thinly sliced lengthwise into ¼-inch-thick strips

1 medium zucchini, cut in half crosswise, then thinly sliced lengthwise into ¼-inch-thick strips

1 red bell pepper, cut into long strips

1 portobello mushroom, stemmed and sliced ½ inch thick

½ red onion, thinly sliced into half-moons

3 tablespoons extra-virgin olive oil

Salt

Ground pepper

1 baguette

Thinly sliced vegan cheese (any flavor; optional)

1 tablespoon balsamic vinegar

Hot sauce (optional)

Preheat the oven to 425 degrees F. Line a large baking sheet with parchment paper.

Put the squash, zucchini, bell pepper, mushroom, and onion in a large bowl. Drizzle 2 tablespoons of the oil over them, season with salt and pepper, and toss until evenly coated. Spread the vegetables on the lined baking sheet in a single layer. Bake for about 30 minutes, until fork-tender.

Slice the baguette crosswise into 4 equal pieces. Slice each piece in half and remove some of the bread from the middle of each half (this makes room for the vegetables). Brush the remaining oil over the cut sides of the bread.

If you are using the optional vegan cheese, put a few slices on the top half of each piece of baguette. Put the cheese-topped bread on another baking sheet and toast in the oven during the last 5 minutes of the veggie roasting time.

Remove the vegetables from the oven. Drizzle the vinegar evenly over them, then gently toss to coat. Taste and add more salt and pepper if desired.

To assemble, divide the vegetables evenly among the bottom halves of the baguette pieces. Sprinkle with hot sauce if desired. Top with the remaining halves of the baguette pieces.

Per serving: 260 calories, 8 g protein, 11 g fat (2 g sat), 31 g carbs, 349 mg sodium, 18 mg calcium, 3 g fiber

This dairy-free pimiento spread tastes way better than its nonvegan counterpart. Since it's made with protein-packed chickpeas and calcium-rich tahini, it's also more wholesome. Slap it on some whole wheat bread for a quick lunch, or spread it on crackers for a tasty snack.

Pimiento Cheese Sandwiches

MAKES 2 1/4 CUPS CHEESE SPREAD; ENOUGH FOR 4 SANDWICHES

1 can (14 to 16 ounces) **chickpeas, drained and rinsed**

1/2 cup chopped roasted red bell pepper

1/4 cup nutritional yeast

1/4 cup vegan mayonnaise or Tofu Mayo (page 8)

2 tablespoons freshly squeezed lemon juice

1 1/2 tablespoons tahini

1 clove garlic, minced

1/4 teaspoon salt

1/4 teaspoon ground cumin

1 jar (2 ounces) **diced pimientos, drained**

8 slices whole wheat or whole-grain sandwich bread

Put the chickpeas, roasted bell pepper, nutritional yeast, vegan mayonnaise, lemon juice, tahini, garlic, salt, and cumin in a food processor. Process until creamy, stopping occasionally to scrape down the work bowl and move the mixture toward the blades. Transfer the mixture to a medium bowl or storage container and stir in the pimientos. Refrigerate until ready to serve. Spread generously on the bread just before serving.

Per sandwich: 250 calories, 12 g protein, 8 g fat (1 g sat), 30 g carbs, 377 mg sodium, 54 mg calcium, 9 g fiber

Everything tastes better slathered in barbecue sauce—veggie dogs, pizza, grilled vegetables, ice cream. Okay, maybe not ice cream. These homemade, veggie-flecked black-eyed pea burgers certainly benefit from tangy homemade barbecue sauce. My recipe for Memphis-Style Barbecue Sauce is on page 12, but feel free to buy premade 'cue sauce if you're feelin' lazy.

BBQ Black-Eyed Pea Burgers

MAKES 4 BURGERS

BURGERS

1 can (14 to 16 ounces) **black-eyed peas, drained and rinsed**

2 teaspoons canola oil

½ cup peeled and grated carrot

½ cup grated zucchini

¼ cup diced red onion

2 cloves garlic, minced

¼ cup quick-cooking rolled oats

¼ cup boiling water

¼ cup plus 2 tablespoons barbecue sauce (homemade, page 12, or store-bought), **plus more for basting**

2 tablespoons nutritional yeast

1 teaspoon liquid smoke

½ teaspoon seasoning salt

½ teaspoon salt

¼ teaspoon ground pepper

¼ cup vital wheat gluten

To make the burgers, preheat the oven to 350 degrees F. Spray a baking sheet with cooking spray or line it with parchment paper.

Put the black-eyed peas in a large bowl and mash with a potato masher or a fork. It's okay to leave a few peas intact, but mash most of them until fairly smooth.

Heat the oil in a medium skillet over medium heat. Add the carrot, zucchini, onion, and garlic and cook, stirring frequently, until the vegetables are tender, 3 to 5 minutes.

Put the oats and boiling water in a small heatproof bowl and mix well. Let stand for 5 minutes.

Transfer the cooked vegetables to the bowl of black-eyed peas and mix well. Add the oat mixture, barbecue sauce, nutritional yeast, liquid smoke, seasoning salt, salt, and pepper and mix well. Add the vital wheat gluten and mix well. You may need to use your hands to incorporate it. The mixture should be a little sticky.

Divide the mixture into 4 equal portions and shape them into balls. Flatten the balls into thin, burger-sized patties and put them on the prepared baking sheet.

Bake for 15 minutes, then carefully flip each burger. They may not hold their shape when you flip them, but you can reshape them after they're flipped. Baste with barbecue sauce and bake for 25 minutes longer.

Per burger (only): 166 calories, 10 g protein, 3 g fat (0 g sat), 23 g carbs, 531 mg sodium, 95 mg calcium, 4 g fiber

BURGER FIXIN'S

4 whole wheat or whole-grain burger buns, split

Vegan mayonnaise or Tofu Mayo (page 8)

Mustard (optional)

Lettuce leaves

Sliced tomato

Thinly sliced red onion

Sliced pickles

To assemble the burgers, spread the buns with vegan mayonnaise and optional mustard as desired. Put the burgers on the buns and add whatever fixin's you like.

Store any leftover burgers in the refrigerator and reheat in a nonstick skillet with extra barbecue sauce. They also freeze well for 2 to 3 months.

hese avocado and sprout sandwiches are more California than Arkansas, but who's complainin'? Even Southerners enjoy an occasional foray into other regional foods. These are perfect for eatin' on the front porch on a hot and humid summer day. Wash 'em down with a glass of sweet tea. Is that Southern enough for you now?

Protein Power Pockets

Advance preparation required   **MAKES 2 TO 4 HELPIN'S**

2 whole wheat or whole-grain pita pockets, cut in half crosswise

½ cup Creamy Tahini Sauce (page 11)**, plus more if desired**

4 slices (8 ounces) **Sweet 'n' Spicy Marinated Tofu** (page 14)

1 avocado, thinly sliced

½ cup sprouts (any kind)

Sriracha sauce (optional)

Preheat the oven to 375 degrees F.

Put the pita pockets on a small baking sheet and toast in the oven for 5 minutes.

Spread about 2 tablespoons of Creamy Tahini Sauce inside each pita half. Stuff each half with 1 slice of the tofu, one-quarter of the avocado, and 2 tablespoons of the sprouts. Spoon in extra Creamy Tahini Sauce and sriracha sauce if desired.

Per serving (based on 3 servings): 466 calories, 20 g protein, 27 g fat (4 g sat), 35 g carbs, 732 mg sodium, 260 mg calcium, 10 g fiber

angy fried green tomato slices and savory marinated tofu are a match made in vegan heaven. Pile them on whole-grain bread spread with a little Creamy Maple-Dijon Sauce and, hot damn, supper's ready. Fry the tomatoes while the tofu is baking so they will be fresh and crispy when it's time to assemble the sandwiches.

Fried Green Tomato and Tofu Sandwiches

See photo facing page 54.

Advance preparation required   **MAKES 4 SANDWICHES**

CREAMY MAPLE-DIJON SAUCE

2 tablespoons Dijon mustard

2 tablespoons vegan mayonnaise or Tofu Mayo (page 8)

2 tablespoons maple syrup

SANDWICH FIXIN'S

8 slices whole wheat or whole-grain bread, toasted

8 slices Fried Green Tomatoes (page 129)

8 slices (1 pound) **Sweet 'n' Spicy Marinated Tofu** (page 14)

To make the sauce, put the mustard, vegan mayonnaise, and maple syrup in a small bowl and stir until thoroughly blended.

To assemble the sandwiches, spread the sauce evenly over the toast. Top 4 slices of the toast with the tomatoes and tofu. Close each sandwich with the remaining toast.

Per sandwich: 510 calories, 23 g protein, 23 g fat (2 g sat), 54 g carbs, 1,169 mg sodium, 230 mg calcium, 7 g fiber

In the South, people eat weird stuff together—like fried chicken and waffles. I'm not sure who figured out that those two foods should grace the same dinner plate, but once you try this tofu chicken and waffle sandwich, you'll want to thank that mysterious and creative person. By the way, waffle sandwiches are the bomb. Seriously. You'll never want plain ol' sandwich bread again.

Fried Tofu Chicken Wafflewiches with Maple-Mustard Sauce

Advance preparation required   **MAKES 2 SANDWICHES**

MAPLE-MUSTARD SAUCE

1 tablespoon Dijon mustard

1 tablespoon maple syrup

1 teaspoon vegan mayonnaise or Tofu Mayo (page 8)

SANDWICH FIXIN'S

4 slices Southern Fried Tofu Chicken (page 90)

4 frozen vegan waffles or Savory Sandwich Waffles (page 141)

4 large slices tomato

½ cup baby spinach or other baby greens, lightly packed

To make the sauce, put the mustard, maple syrup, and vegan mayonnaise in a small bowl and stir until thoroughly blended.

To assemble the sandwiches, spread the sauce evenly over 2 waffles. Top each with 2 slices of the tofu chicken, 2 slices of tomato, and ¼ cup of the greens. Close each sandwich with the remaining waffles.

Per sandwich: 713 calories, 26 g protein, 30 g fat (3 g sat), 81 g carbs, 1,166 mg sodium, 297 mg calcium, 12 g fiber

**N**o faux meat really comes close to the stringy texture of pulled pork in the classic Memphis-style barbecue sandwich. But the combination of shredded carrots and chewy crumbled tempeh comes pretty darn close. When this filling is doused in extra barbecue sauce and piled high on a bun with Creamy Poppy Seed Coleslaw, the result is a true Memphis eatin' experience. Oh, be sure to keep the wet naps handy.

BBQ "Pulled" Tempeh and Carrot Sandwiches

See photo facing page 86.

MAKES 2 SANDWICHES

8 ounces tempeh, crumbled

1 tablespoon canola oil

3 tablespoons minced red onion

2 cloves garlic, minced

2 carrots, peeled and grated

½ cup barbecue sauce (homemade, page 12, or store-bought)**, plus more for spreading**

2 whole wheat or whole-grain buns, split and toasted

½ cup Creamy Poppy Seed Coleslaw (page 52; optional)

Steam the tempeh for 10 minutes.

Heat the oil in a medium skillet over medium-high heat. Add the onion and cook, stirring frequently, for 2 to 3 minutes. Add the garlic and cook, stirring frequently, for 1 minute. Add the carrots and cook, stirring frequently, until the carrots are tender, about 5 minutes.

Add the tempeh and cook, stirring occasionally, until browned, about 5 minutes. Stir in the barbecue sauce and cook, stirring frequently, for 3 to 5 minutes, until heated through.

Divide the mixture evenly between the bottom halves of the buns. Top each sandwich with barbecue sauce as desired and ¼ cup of the optional coleslaw. Top with the remaining halves of the buns.

Per sandwich: 523 calories, 28 g protein, 21 g fat (3 g sat), 51 g carbs, 777 mg sodium, 242 mg calcium, 13 g fiber

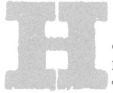

ere's a vegan twist on the BLT, with tofu standing in for the conventional bacon. It's the perfect comfort-food sandwich. I've spiced this version up with a bit of Thai sriracha sauce.

Some-Like-It-Hot TLT

Advance preparation required   **MAKES 2 SANDWICHES**

MARINATED TOFU

8 ounces extra-firm regular tofu, drained and pressed (see page 5)

¼ cup reduced-sodium soy sauce

1 tablespoon hoisin sauce

1 tablespoon maple syrup

1 teaspoon liquid smoke

1 to 2 teaspoons sriracha sauce

SANDWICH FIXIN'S

4 slices whole wheat or whole-grain bread, toasted

Vegan mayonnaise or Tofu Mayo (page 8)

Sriracha sauce

4 large slices tomato

½ avocado, thinly sliced

2 to 4 large leaves romaine lettuce

To make the marinated tofu, slice the tofu into 4 equal slabs. Put the soy sauce, hoisin sauce, maple syrup, liquid smoke, and 1 teaspoon of the sriracha sauce in a small bowl and stir until thoroughly blended. Taste and add more sriracha sauce if desired. Brush both sides of the tofu slabs with the marinade and put them in a storage container. Cover and refrigerate for 8 to 12 hours.

Spray a large skillet with cooking spray. Put the tofu slices in the skillet and cook over medium heat until browned on the bottom, 5 to 7 minutes. Carefully flip the tofu and cook until the other side is browned, about 5 minutes.

To assemble the sandwiches, spread 2 slices of the toast with as much vegan mayonnaise and sriracha sauce as desired. Top each of the other 2 slices of toast with 2 slabs of the cooked tofu, 2 slices of tomato, and half of the avocado and lettuce. Top with the remaining slices of toast, spread-side down.

Per sandwich: 398 calories, 23 g protein, 15 g fat (2 g sat), 44 g carbs, 888 mg sodium, 263 mg calcium, 10 g fiber

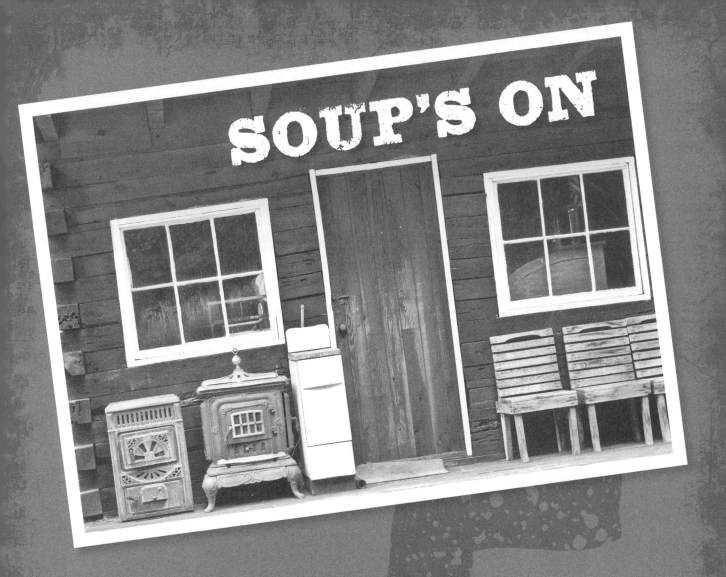

SOUP'S ON

SOUPS AND STEWS

There's nothin' better than a pot of warm soup beans to thaw cold bones on chilly Southern nights. Of course, we don't really know what cold is down here in the South, where snow is a magical thing that might happen once a year—if we're lucky. That's why we think 40 degrees is pretty darn cold.

If you live up someplace where the winters are truly harsh, you'll surely appreciate a steamin' bowl of Chipotle Chickpea Chili (page 76), Country Potato Soup (page 71), or Tempeh Gumbo (page 77) on chill-your-bones winter nights. Some of the other soups, such as Summer's Bounty Veggie Soup (page 70) or Harvest Crowder Peas (page 72), are best enjoyed in the warmer months, when fresh, seasonal produce is abundant.

**W**ho needs that condensed, dairy-laden canned stuff when you can have this homemade vegan cream of mushroom soup? Serve it with a vegan grilled cheese sandwich on a cold winter day, or use it in recipes like Creamy Tofu Chicken Pasta Bake (page 114) or Cheesy Broccoli-Rice Casserole (page 111).

Vegan Cream of Mushroom Soup

MAKES 4 CUPS; 4 HELPIN'S

¼ cup nonhydrogenated vegan margarine

1 pound button mushrooms, sliced

1 teaspoon dried marjoram

1 teaspoon dried tarragon

1 teaspoon dried thyme

½ teaspoon salt, plus more if desired

½ cup cornstarch

4 cups unsweetened soy milk

Melt the margarine in a large saucepan over medium heat. Add the mushrooms, marjoram, tarragon, thyme, and salt and mix well. Cook, stirring frequently, until the mushrooms cook down a bit, 7 to 10 minutes.

Put the cornstarch and soy milk in a medium bowl and stir until the cornstarch is dissolved. Pour into the saucepan and cook, stirring constantly, until the mixture thickens, about 5 minutes. Taste and add more salt if desired.

Leave as is for a chunky mushroom soup. For a smooth, creamy soup, let cool for a few minutes, as blending hot mixtures can be dangerous. Transfer to a blender and process until smooth.

Per cup: 319 calories, 12 g protein, 15 g fat (4 g sat), 31 g carbs, 764 mg sodium, 86 mg calcium, 2 g fiber

y mom created this recipe to use in her famous cornbread dressin' (page 112) so I would be able to enjoy dressin' at the Thanksgiving dinner table. Use it in that recipe, or enjoy a bowl served alongside a vegan grilled cheese sandwich.

Vegan Cream of Celery Soup

MAKES 7 CUPS; 7 HELPIN'S

2 tablespoons nonhydrogenated vegan margarine

1 onion, chopped

8 cloves garlic, minced

2 tablespoons whole wheat pastry flour

12 large stalks celery, chopped

3 medium red potatoes, peeled and diced

4 to 5 cups water

1 teaspoon Greek seasoning salt or other seasoning salt

1 teaspoon dried dill weed

1 teaspoon dried parsley

Salt

Ground pepper

Melt the margarine in a large soup pot over medium heat. Add the onion and cook, stirring frequently, for 3 to 4 minutes. Add the garlic and cook, stirring frequently, for 1 minute. Sprinkle in the flour and stir until the vegetables are evenly coated.

Add the celery and potatoes and enough of the water to cover the potatoes. Stir in the seasoning salt, dill weed, and parsley. Increase the heat to high and bring to a boil. Decrease the heat to medium-low, cover, and simmer until the potatoes are fork-tender, about 20 minutes. Remove from the heat.

Let cool for a few minutes, as blending hot mixtures can be dangerous. Working in batches, transfer to a blender and process until smooth. Combine all of the batches and season with salt and pepper to taste. Reheat before serving if necessary (unless using the soup in another recipe).

Per cup: 126 calories, 2 g protein, 3 g fat (1 g sat), 19 g carbs, 277 mg sodium, 45 mg calcium, 3 g fiber

A ll winter long, we yearn for the juicy sweetness of a farm-fresh summer tomato. Then, at the height of the growing season, we're overwhelmed with them. What to do with all those tomatoes, not to mention the okra, squash, corn, and other abundant produce threatening to overflow the fridge? There's a simple solution: homemade veggie soup. Play around with this recipe and feel free to throw any extra veggies in the pot.

Summer's Bounty Veggie Soup

Advance preparation required   **MAKES 6 TO 8 HELPIN'S**

6 large tomatoes

¾ cup water, plus more if needed

6 cups low-sodium vegetable broth

2 summer squash, sliced

2 cups sliced fresh okra

1 large potato, scrubbed and diced

3 carrots, peeled and sliced

1 yellow onion, diced

1 cup hulled fresh black-eyed peas
   or purplehull peas

Kernels from 1 ear yellow corn

2 stalks celery, chopped

¼ cup chopped fresh basil,
   lightly packed

5 cloves garlic, minced

1 small jalapeño chile, minced

1½ to 3 teaspoons adobo seasoning
   or seasoning salt, plus more
   if desired

1 teaspoon dried oregano

2 bay leaves

Put the tomatoes in a large pot and add just enough water to cover them. Bring to a boil over high heat, then decrease the heat to medium-high and boil for 1 minute. Drain in a colander and run cold water over the tomatoes until they're cool enough to handle. Peel the tomatoes (the skins should slip off easily) and discard the skins. Cut the tomatoes into quarters.

Return the tomatoes to the pot and add the water. Bring to a boil over high heat. Decrease the heat to medium-low, cover, and simmer until the tomatoes are very soft and broken down, 45 to 60 minutes, checking the water level periodically. If the water has cooked off and the tomatoes are sticking, add more water, about ¼ cup at a time. The tomatoes should be thick and saucy, so only add enough water to prevent sticking.

Mash the tomatoes with a potato masher or a fork. Add the broth, squash, okra, potato, carrots, onion, black-eyed peas, corn, celery, basil, garlic, chile, 1½ teaspoons of the adobo seasoning and the oregano and bay leaves and mix well. Bring to a boil over high heat. Decrease the heat to medium-low, cover, and simmer, stirring occasionally, until all the vegetables are tender, 35 to 40 minutes. Taste and add more adobo seasoning if desired.

NOTE: You can also make this soup in a slow cooker. Prepare the tomatoes as directed, then put the tomatoes and all the other ingredients in the slow cooker. Cover and cook on the high setting for 1 hour. Turn the setting to low and cook for 6 to 8 hours longer. Remove the bay leaves before serving.

Per serving (based on 7 servings): 154 calories, 6 g protein, 1 g fat (0 g sat), 28 g carbs, 611 mg sodium, 85 mg calcium, 8 g fiber

ho says vegans have to miss out on creamy soups? Thanks to unsweetened soy milk and whole wheat flour, this hearty soup is more wholesome than its dairy-laden counterpart—and more delicious. Serve this on a cold winter night for instant soul soothing.

Country Potato Soup

MAKES 4 TO 6 HELPIN'S

4 cups peeled and cubed potatoes
(about 2 medium baking potatoes)

1 large carrot, peeled and sliced

2 stalks celery, sliced

1 tablespoon canola oil

1 onion, chopped

1½ cups low-sodium vegetable broth

2 cups unsweetened soy milk

2 tablespoons whole wheat pastry flour

5 slices cooked store-bought vegan bacon (see note), **crumbled**

½ teaspoon salt, plus more if desired

¼ teaspoon ground pepper, plus more if desired

Put the potatoes, carrot, and celery in a large soup pot and add water to cover. Bring to a boil over high heat. Decrease the heat to medium-low and simmer uncovered until the potatoes are fork-tender, about 20 minutes. Drain in a colander.

In the same pot, heat the oil over medium heat. Add the onion and cook, stirring frequently, for 2 to 3 minutes. Add the broth and drained vegetables and mix well.

Put the soy milk and flour in a small bowl and whisk to combine. Pour into the soup pot, increase the heat to medium-high, and cook, stirring constantly, until the mixture comes to a boil. Decrease the heat to medium-low and simmer uncovered, stirring almost constantly, until the soup thickens, 10 to 12 minutes. Stir in the vegan bacon, salt, and pepper. Taste and add more salt and pepper if desired.

NOTE: I call for store-bought vegan bacon here because it's convenient. However, you could substitute Bringin' Home the Tempeh Bacon (page 25) if you like.

Per serving (based on 5 servings): 178 calories, 6 g protein, 7 g fat (1 g sat), 23 g carbs, 432 mg sodium, 57 mg calcium, 3 g fiber

rowder peas are a bit like black-eyed peas, but slightly larger and without the distinctive black eye. Here in the South, crowder peas are abundant at farmers' markets during the height of the summer growing season. If fresh crowder peas aren't available in your area, try substituting fresh black-eyed peas or purplehull peas.

Harvest Crowder Peas

MAKES 4 TO 6 HELPIN'S

1 tablespoon canola oil

½ red onion, chopped

2 cloves garlic, minced

2 stalks celery, diced

1 large carrot, peeled and sliced

4 cups low-sodium vegetable broth

3 cups hulled fresh crowder peas

½ teaspoon salt, plus more if desired

2 tablespoons chopped fresh basil

Heat the oil in a large soup pot over medium heat. Add the onion and cook, stirring frequently, for 2 to 3 minutes. Add the garlic and cook, stirring frequently, for 1 minute. Add the celery and carrot and cook until the vegetables are tender, about 5 minutes.

Add the broth, increase the heat to high, and bring to a boil. Stir in the peas and salt. Decrease the heat to low, cover, and simmer, stirring occasionally, until the peas are tender, 30 to 35 minutes. Taste and add more salt if desired. Remove from the heat and stir in the basil.

Per serving (based on 5 servings): 174 calories, 8 g protein, 3 g fat (0 g sat), 27 g carbs, 353 mg sodium, 59 mg calcium, 8 g fiber

y granny came up with this recipe when she was fiddlin' around in the kitchen. It involves two of my favorite foods—creamy Great Northern beans and iron-rich collards. You can substitute other beans or greens in this recipe, but I love this combination too much to even fathom switching. Crumble a slice of Jalapeño-Corn Buttermilk Cornbread (page 137) into this soup for a quintessential Southern meal.

White Bean and Collard Soup

Advance preparation required   **MAKES 6 TO 8 HELPIN'S**

BEANS

2 cups dried Great Northern beans (about 1 pound), **soaked in water for 8 to 12 hours and drained**

6 cups hot water

1 can (14.5 ounces) **low-sodium diced tomatoes with juice**

1 onion, chopped

2 cloves garlic, minced

1 tablespoon extra-virgin olive oil

½ teaspoon salt

¼ teaspoon ground ginger

¼ teaspoon crushed red pepper flakes

⅛ teaspoon ground nutmeg

GREENS

1 bunch collard greens, stemmed and torn into small pieces

1 cup water

2 teaspoons extra-virgin olive oil

¼ teaspoon salt

Ground pepper

Hot sauce

To make the beans, put all the ingredients in a large soup pot and bring to a boil over high heat. Decrease the heat to medium, partially cover, and cook, stirring occasionally, until very tender, 1½ to 2 hours.

To make the greens, put them in another large pot with the water, oil, salt, and as much pepper and hot sauce as desired. Cover and cook over medium heat, stirring occasionally, until the greens are tender, about 20 minutes.

To assemble the dish, add the cooked greens and their juices (also known as pot likker) to the pot of beans and cook, stirring occasionally, for 10 minutes.

Per serving (based on 7 servings): 127 calories, 7 g protein, 4 g fat (1 g sat), 13 g carbs, 323 mg sodium, 154 mg calcium, 7 g fiber

assolada is a Greek soup made with white beans and vegetables. In this recipe, the addition of kale gives the soup a Southern flair. After all, we do love our greens down here in the South.

Southern Fassolada

Advance preparation required

MAKES 6 TO 8 HELPIN'S

2 cups dried Great Northern beans (about 1 pound), **soaked in water for 8 to 12 hours and drained**

6 cups hot water

1 tablespoon extra-virgin olive oil

1 white onion, chopped

1 red bell pepper, chopped

2 cups chopped kale, packed

2 tablespoons chopped fresh basil

½ teaspoon salt, plus more if desired

½ teaspoon Greek seasoning salt or other seasoning salt

½ teaspoon dried dill weed

¼ teaspoon ground pepper, plus more if desired

Put the beans in a large soup pot. Add the hot water and bring to a boil over high heat. Cover and decrease the heat to medium-low.

Heat the oil in a medium skillet over medium heat. Add the onion and cook, stirring frequently, for 2 to 3 minutes. Add the bell pepper and cook, stirring frequently, until the pepper is tender, 3 to 5 minutes.

Add the onion mixture, kale, basil, salt, seasoning salt, dill weed, and pepper to the beans and mix well. Cover and simmer, stirring occasionally, until the beans are very tender, 1½ to 2 hours. Taste and add more salt and pepper if desired.

NOTE: You can also make this soup in a slow cooker. Just put all the ingredients in the slow cooker. Cover and cook on the high setting for 3 hours. Turn the setting to low and cook for 6 hours longer.

Per serving (based on 7 servings): 99 calories, 5 g protein, 2 g fat (0 g sat), 11 g carbs, 346 mg sodium, 68 mg calcium, 5 g fiber

 **N**othing goes better with split peas than pearl barley, except maybe smoke flavor. Fortunately, you get both of these in this hearty, warming soup. Don't let the heat of the chipotles scare you. When it's cold outside, few things warm you to the bone better than spicy food. Serve this with a big ol' garden salad and a slice of cornbread for the perfect winter meal.

Smoky Chipotle Pea Soup

MAKES 6 TO 8 HELPIN'S

2¼ cups water

¾ cup pearl barley

1 tablespoon canola oil

1 onion, chopped

2 cloves garlic, minced

2 carrots, peeled and sliced

2 stalks celery, diced

2 to 3 canned chipotle chiles in
    adobo sauce, diced

8 cups low-sodium vegetable broth

2½ cups dried split peas (about
    1 pound)

2 teaspoons liquid smoke

1 teaspoon adobo sauce from the
    canned chipotle chiles

1 teaspoon dried rosemary

2 bay leaves

Salt

Ground pepper

Bring the water to a boil in a medium saucepan over high heat. Stir in the barley and return to a boil. Decrease the heat to low, cover, and cook until the barley is tender and the liquid is absorbed, about 45 minutes.

Heat the oil in a large soup pot over medium heat. Add the onion and cook, stirring frequently, for 2 to 3 minutes. Add the garlic and cook, stirring frequently, for 1 minute. Add the carrots, celery, and chiles and cook until the vegetables are tender, about 5 minutes.

Add the broth, split peas, liquid smoke, adobo sauce, rosemary, and bay leaves and mix well. Increase the heat to high and bring to a boil. Decrease the heat to low, cover, and simmer, stirring occasionally, until the split peas are tender, 20 to 25 minutes. Remove from the heat and stir in 2 cups of the barley (reserve any leftover barley for another meal). Season with salt and pepper to taste. Remove the bay leaves before serving

Per serving (based on 7 servings): 220 calories, 9 g protein, 3 g fat (0 g sat), 31 g carbs, 578 mg sodium, 59 mg calcium, 12 g fiber

chickpeas, kidney beans, and tofu pack in the protein in this hearty one-pot meal. The addition of smoky chipotle chiles is the final touch in creating a satisfying dish that's perfect for taking the chill out of an icy winter freeze.

Chipotle Chickpea Chili

MAKES 4 TO 6 HELPIN'S

1 tablespoon canola oil

1 onion, chopped

3 cloves garlic, minced

8 button mushrooms, sliced

8 ounces extra-firm regular tofu, drained and cubed

1 canned chipotle chile in adobo sauce, minced

1 can (28 ounces) low-sodium diced tomatoes with juice

1 can (14 to 16 ounces) chickpeas, drained and rinsed

1 can (14 to 16 ounces) kidney beans, drained and rinsed

½ cup frozen corn kernels

2 tablespoons no-salt-added tomato paste

2 tablespoons chili powder

1 teaspoon adobe sauce from the canned chipotle chiles

½ teaspoon salt

¼ teaspoon ground cumin

Heat the oil in a large soup pot over medium heat. Add the onion and cook, stirring frequently, for 2 to 3 minutes. Add the garlic and mushrooms and cook, stirring occasionally, until the mushrooms begin to cook down, 5 to 7 minutes.

Add the tofu and chile and cook, stirring frequently, until the tofu is lightly browned, 5 to 7 minutes. Add the tomatoes and their juice and the chickpeas, kidney beans, corn, tomato paste, chili powder, adobo sauce, salt, and cumin and stir well. Decrease the heat to low, cover, and simmer, stirring occasionally, for 30 minutes.

Per serving (based on 7 servings): 220 calories, 9 g protein, 3 g fat (0 g sat), 31 g carbs, 578 mg sodium, 59 mg calcium, 12 g fiber

he key to a successful New Orleans gumbo is a thick roux, which is a combination of flour and fat—in this case canola oil—cooked until browned and toasty. Be patient with the roux-makin' step. When you take that first bite of hearty, spicy gumbo, you'll understand why you did.

Tempeh Gumbo

See photo facing page 87.

MAKES 6 HELPIN'S

⅓ cup plus 1 tablespoon canola oil

1 onion, chopped

2 cloves garlic, minced

8 ounces tempeh, cubed

2 stalks celery, chopped

1 green bell pepper, chopped

½ cup whole wheat pastry flour

6 cups low-sodium vegetable broth

1 can (28 ounces) **no-salt-added stewed tomatoes with juice**

2 cups sliced fresh okra

½ cup chopped fresh parsley, lightly packed

2 teaspoons dried thyme

½ teaspoon Cajun seasoning

½ teaspoon cayenne

2 bay leaves

Salt

Ground pepper

Heat 1 tablespoon of the oil in a large skillet over medium heat. Add the onion and cook, stirring frequently, for 2 to 3 minutes. Add the garlic and cook, stirring frequently, for 1 minute. Add the tempeh and cook, stirring frequently, until browned all over, about 5 minutes. Add the celery and bell pepper and cook, stirring frequently, until tender, about 5 minutes.

Heat ⅓ cup of the oil in a large soup pot over low heat. Gradually add the flour, stirring it in 1 to 2 tablespoons at a time. After all the flour is added, continue to cook, stirring constantly, until the mixture turns dark brown, about 10 minutes. Stir in the broth. Add the tempeh mixture, the tomatoes and their juice, and the okra, parsley, thyme, Cajun seasoning, cayenne, and bay leaves and mix well. Increase the heat to high and bring to a boil. Decrease the heat to medium, cover, and cook, stirring occasionally, until the vegetables are tender, about 30 minutes. Season with salt and pepper to taste. Remove the bay leaves before serving.

Per serving: 319 calories, 11 g protein, 18 g fat (2 g sat), 26 g carbs, 185 mg sodium, 172 mg calcium, 7 g fiber

Remember that beef stew in a can? It's so fattening and meaty, but in my prevegan childhood days, it was such comfort food. Nothing satisfies like a steamy bowl of chunky stew.

Seitan Beef Stew

2 cups bite-sized chunks seitan
  or Seitan Beef (page 17)

½ cup whole wheat pastry flour

1 tablespoon canola oil

1 onion, chopped

2 cloves garlic, minced

5 cups low-sodium vegetable broth

3 cups chopped kale, packed

1 large baking potato, peeled
  and cubed

2 carrots, peeled and sliced

3 tablespoons no-salt-added
  tomato paste

1 teaspoon dried marjoram

½ teaspoon dried rosemary

½ teaspoon salt

¼ teaspoon ground pepper

¼ cup water

2 tablespoons cornstarch

Put the seitan in a medium bowl. Sprinkle the flour over the top and stir until evenly coated.

Heat the oil in a large soup pot over medium heat. Add the onion and cook, stirring frequently, for 2 to 3 minutes. Add the garlic and cook, stirring frequently, for 1 minute. Add the seitan and cook, stirring frequently, until browned, about 5 minutes. The seitan may stick to the pot a little, but that's okay; the crispy bits from the bottom of the pot will only make the stew taste better.

Stir in the broth. Add the kale, potato, carrots, tomato paste, marjoram, rosemary, salt, and pepper. Increase the heat to high and bring to a boil. Decrease the heat to medium-low, cover, and simmer, stirring occasionally, until the potato and carrots are fork-tender, 15 to 20 minutes.

Put the water and cornstarch in a small bowl and stir until the cornstarch is dissolved. Pour into the soup pot and simmer, stirring almost constantly, until the stew is thickened, 5 to 7 minutes.

Per serving (based on 5.5 servings): 235 calories, 17 g protein, 4 g fat (0 g sat), 32 g carbs, 556 mg sodium, 129 mg calcium, 6 g fiber

COME 'N' GET IT

SIMPLE SOUTHERN SUPPERS

The term "dinner" causes a little confusion in some parts of the South since the word is often interchangeable with "lunch." My dad always refers to his midday meal as "dinner." For the sake of clearing up mealtime confusion, let's just call the last meal of the day "supper."

Most of the entrées in this chapter are veganized versions of traditional Southern meat-based entrées, made animal-friendly and more healthful with tofu, tempeh, seitan, and various faux meat products. Seitan Tips over Brown Rice (page 97) is a meat-free spin on the classic beef tips dish, while Country-Fried Tempeh Steak with Soy Milk Gravy (page 94) gives us vegans a chance to enjoy a "chicken-fried" supper without any birds paying the price. As an homage to my home city, Memphis, I've also included plenty of barbecue-influenced dishes, such as BBQ Tempeh Pizza (page 103), BBQ Tofu Spaghetti (page 82), and BBQ Dry Rub Seitan Ribs (page 96).

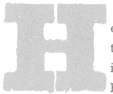ere's a unique variation on New Orleans shrimp creole, with cauliflower making a tasty stand-in for the shrimp. I've included this dish in the entrée section because it makes a satisfying vegetable-based main dish when served over brown rice, but feel free to serve it as a side dish if you like.

Cauliflower Creole

MAKES 4 TO 6 HELPIN'S

1 large head cauliflower, cut into bite-sized florets

2 tablespoons canola oil

Salt

Ground pepper

1 onion, chopped

1 yellow bell pepper, chopped

2 stalks celery, chopped

3 cloves garlic, minced

1½ cups water

1 can (8 ounces) **no-salt-added tomato sauce**

2 tablespoons **no-salt-added tomato paste**

1 teaspoon Cajun seasoning

1 teaspoon dried thyme

1 bay leaf

2 cups cooked brown rice (see note, page 111), **kept warm**

Hot sauce

Preheat the oven to 400 degrees F.

Put the cauliflower in a large bowl. Drizzle with 1 tablespoon of the oil and toss until evenly coated. Season with salt and pepper and toss again. Transfer to a baking sheet and bake for 25 to 30 minutes, stirring and turning halfway through the baking time.

Heat the remaining tablespoon of oil in a large saucepan over medium heat. Add the onion and cook, stirring frequently, for 2 to 3 minutes. Add the bell pepper, celery, and garlic and cook, stirring frequently, until the vegetables are tender, about 10 minutes.

Stir in the water, tomato sauce, tomato paste, Cajun seasoning, thyme, and bay leaf. Increase the heat to high and bring to a boil. Decrease the heat to medium-low and simmer, stirring occasionally, for 5 to 7 minutes. Stir in the cauliflower and cook, stirring occasionally, for 5 to 7 minutes.

Remove the bay leaf and spoon the mixture over individual servings of the rice. Pass the hot sauce at the table.

Per serving (based on 5 servings): 186 calories, 5 g protein, 6 g fat (1 g sat), 26 g carbs, 90 mg sodium, 50 mg calcium, 4 g fiber

This fresh, made-from-scratch pasta sauce takes advantage of abundant summer produce, such as juicy tomatoes, tender zucchini, and sweet yellow bell peppers. I recommend only making this recipe when these vegetables are at the peak of their season. Of course, you can always make an extra batch in summer and freeze it to enjoy during winter.

Spaghetti with Raid-the-Garden Marinara

Advance preparation required   MAKES 3 TO 4 HELPIN'S

8 large tomatoes

1 cup water, plus more if needed

8 ounces whole wheat spaghetti

1 tablespoon extra-virgin olive oil

½ cup chopped red onion

3 cloves garlic, minced

1 cup diced zucchini

1 cup diced yellow bell pepper

½ teaspoon sugar

½ teaspoon dried oregano

¼ cup chopped fresh basil, lightly packed

1 tablespoon red wine (optional)

Salt

Ground pepper

Put the tomatoes in a large pot and add just enough water to cover them. Bring to a boil over high heat, then decrease the heat to medium-high and boil for 1 minute. Drain in a colander and run cold water over the tomatoes until they're cool enough to handle. Peel the tomatoes (the skins should slip off easily) and discard the skins. Cut the tomatoes into quarters.

Return the tomatoes to the pot and add the water. Bring to a boil over high heat. Decrease the heat to medium-low, cover, and simmer until the tomatoes are very soft and broken down, 45 to 60 minutes, checking the water level periodically. If the water has cooked off and the tomatoes are sticking, add more water, about ¼ cup at a time. The tomatoes should be thick and saucy, so only add enough water to prevent sticking.

Bring a large pot of salted water to a boil over high heat. Stir in the spaghetti. Decrease the heat to medium-low and cook, stirring occasionally, until tender but firm. Drain well and return the spaghetti to the pot.

Meanwhile, heat the oil in a large saucepan over medium heat. Add the onion and cook, stirring frequently, for 2 to 3 minutes. Add the garlic and cook, stirring frequently, for 1 minute. Add the zucchini and bell pepper and cook, stirring frequently, until the vegetables just start to soften, 3 to 5 minutes. Add the tomatoes, sugar, and oregano and cook, stirring occasionally, until the vegetables are tender, 10 to 15 minutes. Remove from the heat and stir in the basil and optional wine. Season with salt and pepper to taste.

Pour the sauce over the spaghetti and toss gently until evenly combined.

Per serving (based on 3.5 servings): 341 calories, 13 g protein, 5 g fat (1 g sat), 59 g carbs, 35 mg sodium, 55 mg calcium, 7 g fiber

L egend has it that barbecue spaghetti was developed in Memphis, and I'm inclined to believe it since my city is the self-professed 'cue capital of the country. The combination of tangy barbecue sauce and spaghetti noodles may sound strange, but trust me: it's awesome.

BBQ Tofu Spaghetti

MAKES 3 TO 4 HELPIN'S

8 ounces whole wheat spaghetti

1 tablespoon canola oil

1 cup diced green bell pepper

1 cup diced cremini mushrooms

1 pound extra-firm regular tofu, drained and pressed (see page 5)

1 tablespoon reduced-sodium soy sauce

¾ to 1 cup barbecue sauce (homemade, page 12, or store-bought)

Bring a large pot of salted water to a boil over high heat. Break the spaghetti noodles in half and stir them into the boiling water. Decrease the heat to medium-low and cook, stirring occasionally, until tender but firm. Drain well.

Meanwhile, heat the oil in a large skillet over medium heat. Add the bell pepper and cook, stirring frequently, for 5 minutes. Add the mushrooms and cook, stirring frequently, until the vegetables are tender, about 3 minutes.

Crumble the tofu into the skillet and mix well. Drizzle with the soy sauce, then stir until well combined. Cook, stirring frequently, until the tofu is lightly browned, about 3 minutes. Add ½ cup of the barbecue sauce and cook, stirring frequently, until heated through, about 1 minute.

To serve, portion the spaghetti into shallow bowls. Spoon the tofu mixture over the spaghetti, dividing it evenly among the bowls. Drizzle 1 to 2 tablespoons of the remaining barbecue sauce over each serving.

Per serving (based on 3.5 servings): 476 calories, 26 g protein, 11 g fat (1 g sat), 70 g carbs, 626 mg sodium, 305 mg calcium, 5 g fiber

**E**ven gluten-free vegans can enjoy this alternative to grain-based spaghetti. Spaghetti squash tastes a little like yellow summer squash, but once it's baked and the strands are separated, it looks more like angel hair pasta. Savory pan-fried tofu, cherry tomatoes, and fresh basil offer a simple alternative to marinara sauce, allowing the flavor of the squash to shine.

Spaghetti Squash with Tomatoes and Tofu

MAKES 4 HELPIN'S

1 **spaghetti squash** (2½ to 3 pounds)

1 **pound extra-firm regular tofu,**
 drained and pressed (see page 5)

2 **teaspoons canola oil**

2 **cloves garlic, minced**

½ **teaspoon adobo seasoning or**
 seasoning salt, plus more
 if desired

½ **teaspoon onion powder**

¼ **teaspoon garlic powder**

1 **tablespoon nonhydrogenated**
 vegan margarine

20 **cherry or grape tomatoes, halved**

2 **tablespoons chopped fresh basil**

Salt

Ground pepper

Preheat the oven to 400 degrees F. Spray a large baking sheet with cooking spray.

Cut the spaghetti squash in half lengthwise. Scoop out the seeds and stringy bits with a large metal spoon and discard. Put the squash on the prepared baking sheet cut-side down and bake for about 45 minutes, until the skin can be easily pierced with a fork. Let cool briefly.

When cool enough to handle, scoop around the outer edges of the skin with a large metal spoon to remove the flesh (similar to scooping out an avocado). The flesh should naturally separate into noodle-like strands. If portions remain in clumps, separate them as best you can with a fork. Transfer to a bowl. (The squash may be prepared up to 2 days in advance and stored in a covered container in the refrigerator.)

Cut the tofu into bite-sized cubes.

Heat the oil in a medium skillet over medium heat. Add the tofu and garlic and stir gently to coat the tofu with the oil. Increase the heat to high. Sprinkle in the adobo seasoning, onion powder, and garlic powder and stir gently to coat the tofu with the spices. Cook without stirring until the cubes are browned on the bottom. Stir, then cook without stirring until browned again, about 5 minutes longer. Remove from the heat.

Melt the margarine in a large, deep skillet over medium heat. Add the squash and stir to coat. Cook, stirring occasionally, until heated through, about 5 minutes. Add the tofu, tomatoes, and basil and stir gently until evenly combined. Cook, occasionally stirring gently, until heated through, about 5 minutes. Season with salt, pepper, and more adobo seasoning to taste if desired.

Per serving: 272 calories, 16 g protein, 12 g fat (2 g sat), 24 g carbs, 446 mg sodium, 278 mg calcium, 7 g fiber

For me, the hardest part of going vegan was the thought of giving up that comforting bowl of creamy macaroni and cheese. But thanks to millions of enterprising vegan cooks, there are lots of recipes for dairy-free mac and cheese. Mine uses a creamy cashew and nutritional yeast sauce in place of the traditional sauce made with milk and dairy cheese.

Creamy Cashew Mac and Cheese

MAKES 4 TO 6 HELPIN'S

8 ounces quinoa macaroni or whole wheat macaroni

1 tablespoon nonhydrogenated vegan margarine

½ cup chopped onion

2 cloves garlic, minced

1 cup raw cashews

1 cup unsweetened soy milk, plus more if desired

½ cup nutritional yeast

2 tablespoons freshly squeezed lemon juice

½ teaspoon salt

¼ teaspoon dry mustard

Ground pepper

½ cup shredded vegan Cheddar cheese (optional)

Bring a large pot of salted water to a boil over high heat. Stir in the macaroni. Decrease the heat to medium-low and cook, stirring occasionally, until tender but firm. Drain well.

Meanwhile, melt the margarine in a small skillet over medium heat. Add the onion and cook, stirring frequently, for 4 to 5 minutes. Add the garlic and cook, stirring frequently, for 1 minute. Remove from the heat.

Put the cashews, onion mixture, ¼ cup of the soy milk, and the nutritional yeast, lemon juice, salt, mustard, and as much pepper as desired in a food processor. Process until very creamy, 3 to 5 minutes, stopping occasionally to scrape down the work bowl and move the mixture toward the blades.

Pour the cashew mixture into a large saucepan. Stir in the remaining ¾ cup of soy milk and the optional vegan cheese. Cook over medium-low heat, stirring occasionally, until heated through and the cheese is melted, about 5 minutes. Remove from the heat.

Add the macaroni and stir gently until well combined. Add more soy milk if needed to achieve the desired creaminess.

Per serving (based on 5 servings): 395 calories, 17 g protein, 17 g fat (3 g sat), 48 g carbs, 266 mg sodium, 48 mg calcium, 4 g fiber

Cheeseburger macaroni from a box ain't got nothin' on the veganized version of this homey comfort dish.

Cheesy Burger Mac

8 ounces quinoa macaroni or whole wheat macaroni

1¼ cups frozen veggie burger crumbles, thawed, or Ground TSP Beef (page 18)

1½ cups Basic Cheesy Sauce (page 13)

½ cup shredded vegan Cheddar cheese (optional)

Bring a large pot of salted water to a boil over high heat. Stir in the macaroni. Decrease the heat to medium-low and cook, stirring occasionally, until tender but firm. Drain well and return the macaroni to the pot.

Meanwhile, spray a medium skillet with cooking spray. If using veggie burger crumbles, put them in the skillet and cook over medium heat, stirring frequently, until the crumbles have browned, 7 to 10 minutes; skip this step if using Ground TSP Beef.

Add the crumbles and cheesy sauce to the pot of cooked macaroni and stir gently until evenly combined. Add the optional vegan cheese and stir gently until it melts. If the cheese doesn't melt completely, put the pot over low heat and cook, stirring gently, until the cheese is melted, 1 to 2 minutes.

Per serving (based on 4.5 servings): 366 calories, 28 g protein, 4 g fat (1 g sat), 58 g carbs, 818 mg sodium, 97 mg calcium, 7 g fiber

Tempeh Gumbo, *page 77*

In the mid-1990s stuffed bell peppers were one of my mom's signature weeknight suppers. She filled them with a mixture of white rice, cheese, ground beef, and spices to make a hearty and flavorful filling for boiled green bell peppers. No offense to Mom, but there's a more healthful way to stuff a pepper. My version has a similar flavor and is equally satisfying, but it's packed with nutrients from protein-rich quinoa, textured soy protein, and nutritional yeast.

Quinoa-Stuffed Bell Peppers

MAKES 4 HELPIN'S

4 large green bell peppers

1 tablespoon canola oil

1 onion, chopped

2 cloves garlic, minced

2 cups low-sodium vegetable broth

1 can (14.5 ounces) **low-sodium diced tomatoes with juice**

1 cup quinoa

¾ cup dry TSP crumbles (see page 5)

1 tablespoon reduced-sodium soy sauce

1 tablespoon vegan Worcestershire sauce (homemade, page 10, or store-bought)

1 teaspoon dried oregano

½ teaspoon dried marjoram

½ teaspoon dried basil

2 tablespoons nutritional yeast

Salt

Ground pepper

Hot sauce

½ cup shredded vegan Cheddar cheese or nutritional yeast (optional)

Preheat the oven to 350 degrees F.

Cut the tops off the bell peppers and remove the seeds. Discard the tops. Steam the peppers cut-side down for 10 minutes. Steamer baskets vary in size, as do the pots they fit in, so the lid may not totally cover the peppers, but that's okay; just balance the lid atop the peppers, leaving a little open space.

Heat the oil in a large saucepan over medium heat. Add the onion and cook, stirring frequently, for 2 to 3 minutes. Add the garlic and cook, stirring frequently, for 1 minute. Add the broth, tomatoes with their juice, quinoa, TSP, soy sauce, Worcestershire sauce, oregano, marjoram, basil, and nutritional yeast. Increase the heat to high and bring to a boil. Decrease the heat to medium-low, cover, and cook until quinoa is tender and most of the liquid is absorbed, 20 to 25 minutes. The mixture should be moist. Season with salt, pepper, and hot sauce to taste.

Spoon about 1 cup of the quinoa mixture into each steamed pepper. If the pepper won't hold a full cup, just fill it to the top (reserve any leftover filling and serve it as a side dish at another meal).

Put the peppers in a deep baking pan or casserole dish, preferably one in which they'll fit somewhat snugly so they remain upright. Top each with 2 tablespoons of the optional vegan cheese if desired. Bake for 20 to 25 minutes, until the filling is heated through and the vegan cheese is melted.

Per serving: 318 calories, 19 g protein, 6 g fat (1 g sat), 44 g carbs, 714 mg sodium, 116 mg calcium, 9 g fiber

Catfish-frying parties are a common occurrence down South, where they're known as "fish fries." Folks get together on Friday or Saturday night to drink beer and toss hush puppies and cornmeal-dredged catfish into a deep fryer in the backyard. This recipe uses tofu "fish" that's neither fish nor fried. Instead, it gets a fishy flavor from dulse flakes. To throw a vegan (and more healthful) "fish fry," bake up some Hush Puppy Corn Muffins (page 139) to serve with this dish.

Baked Tofu Fish Fry

Advance preparation required   **MAKES 4 HELPIN'S**

MARINATED TOFU FISH

1 pound extra-firm regular tofu, drained and pressed (see page 5)

2 cups low-sodium vegetable broth

2 tablespoons reduced-sodium soy sauce

2 tablespoons freshly squeezed lemon juice

1 tablespoon dulse flakes (see notes)

BREADING

¾ cup cornstarch

1 tablespoon dulse flakes (see notes)

½ teaspoon salt

½ teaspoon ground pepper

½ cup unsweetened soy milk

1 cup panko breadcrumbs

To make the marinated tofu fish, cut the block of tofu vertically to form 2 squares or rectangles. Turn each on end and slice into 3 thinner squares. Cut the resulting 6 pieces on the diagonal to make 2 triangles per square, yielding 12 triangle-shaped pieces in all.

Put the broth, soy sauce, lemon juice, and dulse flakes in a large, shallow storage container and mix well. Put the tofu in the marinade and gently flip the triangles over to evenly coat them with the marinade. Cover and refrigerate for 8 to 12 hours, gently turning the tofu once or twice during the marinating time.

Preheat the oven to 350 degrees F. Spray a baking sheet with cooking spray or line it with parchment paper.

To coat the tofu fish in the breading, put the cornstarch, dulse flakes, salt, and pepper in a wide, shallow bowl and mix well. Put the soy milk in another wide, shallow bowl. Put the panko in a third wide, shallow bowl.

Dredge a tofu triangle in the cornstarch mixture, coating both sides, then dip it in the soy milk. Put it in the bowl with the panko and press firmly to ensure the panko sticks, then turn it over and coat the other side with panko in the same way. Put the triangle on the prepared baking sheet. Repeat the process with the remaining tofu, leaving a little space between the triangles.

Bake for 40 minutes, until lightly browned, carefully flipping the tofu halfway through the baking time.

Per serving: 382 calories, 19 g protein, 10 g fat (1 g sat), 51 g carbs, 737 mg sodium, 228 mg calcium, 2 g fiber

TARTAR SAUCE

¼ **cup vegan mayonnaise or Tofu Mayo** (page 8)

1 **tablespoon prepared white horseradish** (see notes)

1 **tablespoon dill pickle relish, drained**

To make the tartar sauce, put all the ingredients in a small bowl and mix well. Serve as a dipping sauce alongside the tofu fish.

NOTES

- Dulse is a mineral-rich sea vegetable that lends this dish a fresh-from-the-sea taste. I'm generally not a fan of fishy-tasting foods, but dulse flakes have a mild flavor that pleases my discerning palate. Look for dulse flakes in the spice section or with the Asian foods at supermarkets or natural food stores.

- Many brands of horseradish contain mayonnaise or dairy products. However, some, such as Bubbie's or Gold's Prepared Horseradish, are vegan. Look for them in the refrigerated section of well-stocked natural food stores and supermarkets.

o vegan Southern cookbook would be complete without a recipe for fried faux chicken. Colonel Sanders would doubtless be green with envy over a bucket of this beer-battered goodness, so let's keep this "secret recipe" just between us.

Southern Fried Tofu Chicken

Advance preparation required   **MAKES 8 SLICES; 4 HELPIN'S**

1⅔ cups whole wheat pastry flour

1 teaspoon garlic powder

1 teaspoon paprika

¼ teaspoon poultry seasoning

½ teaspoon salt, plus more
    for sprinkling

Ground pepper

¾ cup vegan beer (see note)

¼ cup canola oil, plus more if needed

1 pound Tofu Chicken (page 15),
    marinated but not baked, drained

Put 1 cup of the flour in a wide, shallow bowl. Add the garlic powder, paprika, poultry seasoning, ¼ teaspoon of the salt, and as much pepper as desired and mix well.

Put the beer, the remaining ⅔ cup of flour, the remaining ¼ teaspoon of salt, and as much pepper as desired in another wide, shallow bowl and whisk until thoroughly blended.

Line a plate with several layers of paper towels.

Put the oil in a large, heavy skillet over medium heat. The oil should generously coat the bottom of the skillet; if it doesn't, add more oil as needed, 1 tablespoon at a time. Sprinkle a pinch of flour over the oil to check the heat. If the oil sizzles, it's ready.

Gently dredge a slice of the tofu in the seasoned flour mixture, coating both sides evenly. Dip the coated slice in the beer mixture, then dredge it in the seasoned flour mixture again. Carefully lower it into the skillet. Repeat until the skillet is full but not overcrowded; the slices shouldn't touch or overlap. You may have to fry the tofu in two or three batches.

Fry the tofu until golden brown on the bottom, 3 to 5 minutes. Gently turn and fry until golden brown on the other side, 3 to 5 minutes. Transfer to the lined plate to drain. Sprinkle with salt to taste.

NOTE: You can use any type of vegan beer for this recipe, but I recommend using a high-quality amber ale or dark stout. For a comprehensive list of vegan beers, go to barnivore.com.

Per serving (2 slices): 455 calories, 19 g protein, 21 g fat (2 g sat), 45 g carbs, 590 mg sodium, 238 mg calcium, 8 g fiber

There's something magical about finger food. It evokes fond memories of eating like a five-year-old. Times were simpler then, and we didn't need to bother with silly utensils. Plus, handheld food means one less fork to wash. Indulge your inner toddler with these fun stix. I love to dip 'em in barbecue sauce, ketchup seasoned with a little curry powder, marinara sauce, or Dijon mustard sweetened with a few drops of maple syrup.

Cornmeal-Crusted Tofu Stix

Advance preparation required

1 pound Tofu Chicken (page 15), with the tofu cut into 8 fingers and marinated but not baked

¾ cup unsweetened soy milk

1 tablespoon cider vinegar

1 cup yellow cornmeal

½ cup dry whole wheat breadcrumbs

1 tablespoon dried onion flakes

2 teaspoons paprika

1 teaspoon garlic powder

½ teaspoon Cajun seasoning

½ teaspoon ground pepper

¼ teaspoon adobo seasoning or seasoning salt

Preheat the oven to 350 degrees F. Spray a baking sheet with cooking spray or line it with parchment paper.

Put the soy milk and vinegar in a wide, shallow bowl and stir well. Set aside until the soy milk curdles and thickens, about 2 minutes.

Put the cornmeal, breadcrumbs, onion flakes, paprika, garlic powder, Cajun seasoning, pepper, and adobo seasoning in another wide, shallow bowl and mix well.

Remove the tofu from the marinade and discard the marinade. Dip each piece of tofu in the soy milk mixture, then dredge it in the cornmeal mixture until evenly coated on all sides, pressing gently to ensure the cornmeal mixture sticks to the tofu. Put the tofu on the prepared baking sheet. Repeat the process with the remaining tofu, leaving a little space between the pieces.

Bake for 30 minutes, until lightly browned and crispy, carefully flipping the tofu halfway through the baking time.

Per serving: 259 calories, 17 g protein, 7 g fat (1 g sat), 31 g carbs, 531 mg sodium, 191 mg calcium, 4 g fiber

his down-home dish was adapted from a recipe entitled "Tangy Pork Chops" in an old spiral-bound church cookbook in my mom's vast cookbook collection. Serve this dish over brown rice or your favorite whole-grain pasta.

Tangy Tempeh Chops with Green Peppers

Advance preparation required   **MAKES 4 HELPIN'S**

MARINATED TEMPEH

8 ounces tempeh

1 cup water

3 tablespoons reduced-sodium soy sauce

2 tablespoons nutritional yeast

1 tablespoon brown sugar

1 teaspoon onion powder

TEMPEH CHOPS

1 tablespoon canola oil

1 small yellow onion, chopped

1 green bell pepper, cut into large pieces

2 stalks celery, chopped

1 can (14.5 ounces) **no-salt-added stewed tomatoes**

½ cup ketchup

2 tablespoons cider vinegar

2 tablespoons vegan Worcestershire sauce (homemade, page 10, or store-bought)

1 tablespoon sugar

1 tablespoon freshly squeezed lemon juice

Ground pepper

¼ cup water

2 tablespoons cornstarch

To make the marinated tempeh, cut the tempeh in half, then cut each half into 8 strips. Steam for 10 minutes.

Put the water, soy sauce, nutritional yeast, brown sugar, and onion powder in a large, shallow storage container and stir until the sugar is dissolved.

Put the tempeh in the container and gently flip the strips over to evenly coat them with the marinade. Cover and refrigerate for 8 to 12 hours, gently turning the tempeh once or twice during the marinating time.

To make the tempeh chops, heat the oil in a large skillet or saucepan over medium heat. Add the onion and cook, stirring frequently, for 2 to 3 minutes. Add the bell pepper and celery and cook, stirring frequently, until the vegetables begin to soften, 5 to 7 minutes.

Remove the tempeh from the marinade and discard the marinade. Put the tempeh in the skillet and cook, occasionally stirring and turning gently, until the tempeh is brown on both sides, about 10 minutes. Some of the strips may break into pieces, and that's okay.

Put the tomatoes, ketchup, vinegar, Worcestershire sauce, sugar, lemon juice, and as much pepper as desired in a medium bowl and stir until the sugar is dissolved. Pour the mixture into the skillet and cook, occasionally stirring gently, for 15 minutes.

Put the water and cornstarch in a small bowl and mix well. Add to the tempeh mixture and cook, stirring constantly, until the sauce thickens, about 1 minute.

Per serving: 370 calories, 26 g protein, 11 g fat (2 g sat), 44 g carbs, 985 mg sodium, 133 mg calcium, 11 g fiber

Hot wings may have originated in Buffalo, New York, but in Memphis it seems like there's a hot wing joint on every corner. No matter where the dish got its start, hot "wangs" (that's what we call 'em down here) have become a Southern favorite. Since these tasty wangs are actually wing-free, you can scarf 'em down without the guilt. Serve with Country Buttermilk Ranch Dressing (page 9) and celery and carrot sticks. You can also cook up a double batch and serve 'em as appetizers.

Spicy Seitan Hot Wangs

MAKES 4 HELPIN'S

1 cup whole wheat pastry flour

¼ cup nutritional yeast

½ cup unsweetened soy milk

2 cups seitan chunks, or 8 to 10 wing-sized pieces of Seitan Chicken (page 16)

½ cup nonhydrogenated vegan margarine

½ cup hot sauce

½ teaspoon garlic powder

½ teaspoon onion powder

¼ teaspoon dry mustard

Preheat the oven to 400 degrees F. Spray a baking sheet with cooking spray or line it with parchment paper.

Put the flour and nutritional yeast in a medium bowl and mix well. Pour the soy milk into a small bowl.

Dip a piece of the seitan in the soy milk and then in the flour mixture. Still working with the same piece of seitan, dip it in the soy milk again and then in the flour mixture once more. Put the breaded seitan on the prepared baking sheet. Repeat the process with the remaining seitan, leaving a little space between the pieces.

Bake for 30 minutes, until lightly browned and crispy, flipping the seitan halfway through the baking time.

Melt the margarine in a small saucepan over medium heat. Stir in the hot sauce, garlic powder, onion powder, and mustard. Decrease the heat to medium-low and simmer, stirring occasionally, until heated through, 5 to 7 minutes.

Put 4 or 5 pieces of the seitan in the saucepan and stir until evenly coated. Transfer to a plate using a slotted spoon. Repeat with the remaining seitan. Pour the remaining sauce over the seitan just before serving.

Per serving: 465 calories, 25 g protein, 24 g fat (7 g sat), 370 g carbs, 2,094 mg sodium, 79 mg calcium, 6 g fiber

I've never understood chicken-fried steak. Is it chicken, or is it steak? As it turns out, it's some sort of beef patty that's breaded and deep-fried like chicken. These marinated tempeh steaks get a similar treatment, but I prefer to call them "country-fried" because that sounds so much more appetizing. Smother these babies with soy milk gravy, and Southern roots or not, you'll be whisked away to grandma's country cabin.

Country-Fried Tempeh Steak with Soy Milk Gravy

See photo facing page 22.

Advance preparation required

MAKES 4 HELPIN'S

TEMPEH STEAKS

8 ounces tempeh

1 cup low-sodium vegetable broth

½ cup reduced-sodium soy sauce

1 tablespoon extra-virgin olive oil

1 tablespoon maple syrup

1 tablespoon liquid smoke

1 tablespoon vegan Worcestershire sauce (homemade, page 10, or store-bought)

2 cloves garlic, minced

1 teaspoon onion powder

1 cup whole wheat pastry flour

½ cup nutritional yeast

½ cup dry whole wheat breadcrumbs

1 cup unsweetened soy milk

2 teaspoons cider vinegar

¼ cup canola oil, plus more if needed

To make the tempeh steaks, cut the tempeh in half crosswise, then cut each piece in half horizontally to yield 2 thinner pieces. Steam the tempeh for 10 minutes.

Put the broth, soy sauce, olive oil, maple syrup, liquid smoke, Worcestershire sauce, garlic, and onion powder in a large, shallow storage container. Whisk until thoroughly blended.

Put the tempeh in the container and gently flip the pieces over to evenly coat them with the marinade. Cover and refrigerate for 8 to 12 hours, gently turning the tempeh once or twice during the marinating time.

Put the flour, nutritional yeast, and breadcrumbs in a wide, shallow bowl and mix well. Scoop out ¼ cup of the mixture and set aside.

Put the soy milk and the vinegar in another wide, shallow bowl and stir well. Set aside until the soymilk curdles and thickens, about 2 minutes.

Line a plate with several layers of paper towels.

Heat the canola oil in a large, heavy skillet over medium heat. The oil should generously coat the bottom of the skillet; if it doesn't, add more oil as needed, 1 tablespoon at a time. Sprinkle a pinch of flour over the oil to check the heat. If the oil sizzles, it's ready.

Remove the tempeh from the marinade and discard the marinade. Gently dredge a piece of the tempeh in the flour mixture, coating both sides evenly. Dip it in the soy milk, then dredge it in the flour mixture again. Still working with the same piece of tempeh, dip it in the soy milk again and then in the flour mixture once more. Carefully lower

Per serving: 486 calories, 24 g protein, 25 g fat (3 g sat), 42 g carbs, 793 mg sodium, 138 mg calcium, 9 g fiber

GRAVY

1 to 2 tablespoons canola oil, if needed

¼ cup reserved flour mixture from the Tempeh Steaks

⅓ cup low-sodium vegetable broth

1 cup unsweetened soy milk

½ teaspoon minced fresh sage, or ¼ teaspoon rubbed sage

¼ teaspoon salt

Ground pepper

the tempeh into the skillet. Repeat with the remaining 3 pieces of tempeh, placing each in the skillet as you go.

Fry the tempeh until brown on the bottom, 3 to 5 minutes. Gently turn and fry until brown on the other side, about 3 minutes. Transfer to the lined plate, cover, and let drain. Leave the skillet over the heat.

To make the gravy, use the remaining canola oil in the skillet; if the tempeh absorbed all of the oil, add 1 to 2 more tablespoons of canola oil.

Whisk the reserved flour mixture into the oil. Add the broth and immediately whisk or stir until thoroughly blended and lump-free. Add the soy milk, sage, and salt and cook, stirring constantly, until the mixture thickens, about 5 minutes. Season with pepper to taste. Spoon the gravy over the tempeh steaks just before serving.

COUNTRY-BAKED TEMPEH STEAKS: Marinate the tempeh as directed in the main recipe. Preheat the oven to 350 degrees F. Spray a baking sheet with cooking spray or line it with parchment paper. Coat the tempeh in the flour mixture and soy milk as directed in the main recipe, then put the coated pieces on the prepared baking sheet. Bake for 30 minutes, until crisp and browned, gently flipping the tempeh halfway through the baking time.

To make the gravy, heat 2 tablespoons of canola oil in a small saucepan over medium heat. Follow the instructions in the main recipe for adding the reserved flour mixture, broth, soy milk, sage, salt, and pepper.

I n Memphis folks get pretty worked up over the wet ribs versus dry ribs debate. Some folks prefer their ribs coated with sticky barbecue sauce. Others would rather get the barbecue flavor from a combination of salty and sweet spices rubbed into the ribs. Personally, I like my vegan ribs both ways, but I'm particularly fond of this dry rub version. You won't even need a wet nap after eatin' 'em.

BBQ Dry Rub Seitan Ribs

MAKES 5 HELPIN'S

SEITAN RIBS

1 cup vital wheat gluten

⅓ cup chickpea flour

¼ cup nutritional yeast

½ teaspoon seasoning salt

¾ cup water

¼ cup barbecue sauce (homemade, page 12, or store-bought)

2 tablespoons tahini

1 teaspoon liquid smoke

DRY RUB

1 tablespoon brown sugar

½ teaspoon seasoning salt

½ teaspoon smoked paprika

½ teaspoon garlic powder

½ teaspoon dried thyme

⅛ teaspoon cayenne

⅛ teaspoon ground pepper

To make the seitan ribs, preheat the oven to 350 degrees F. Spray an 8-inch square baking pan with cooking spray.

Put the vital wheat gluten, chickpea flour, nutritional yeast, and seasoning salt in a large bowl and mix well.

Put the water, barbecue sauce, tahini, and liquid smoke in a blender and process until smooth. Pour into the flour mixture and mix well. Knead the dough in the bowl for 5 minutes. It will be wet at first, but as you knead, it will thicken and become quite firm. Let rest for 5 minutes.

To make the dry rub, put all the ingredients in a small bowl and mix well.

To season and bake the ribs, put the dough in the prepared pan and press and stretch it until it covers the bottom of the pan. Cut the dough in half, then cut each of the halves into five 4-inch-long strips.

Sprinkle about one-quarter of the dry rub over the seitan. Lightly press the seasoning into the surface. Sprinkle a little more of the dry rub as needed to coat the seitan well. Turn the strips over and sprinkle about half of the remaining dry rub over the seitan. Lightly press the seasoning into the surface. Sprinkle a little more of the dry rub as needed to coat the seitan well. You may not use all of the rub.

Bake for 25 minutes, until firm and lightly browned, flipping the seitan halfway through the baking time.

Per serving: 187 calories, 22 g protein, 4 g fat (0 g sat), 16 g carbs, 366 mg sodium, 90 mg calcium, 2 g fiber

Omnivores may get their comfort-food kick from hearty beef tips over white rice. But vegans only take comfort when we know no animals are harmed. It also helps when we get some actual nutrients rather than empty calories, so I've substituted brown rice for its whole-grain goodness and seitan for chewy, cruelty-free satisfaction.

Seitan Tips over Brown Rice

MAKES 4 HELPIN'S

2¾ cups water

1 cup brown rice

1 tablespoon canola oil

1 onion, chopped

1 red bell pepper, cut into large pieces

2 cloves garlic, minced

2 cups bite-sized chunks seitan or Seitan Beef (page 17)

10 button mushrooms, sliced

½ cup cooking sherry

1 tablespoon dried parsley

½ teaspoon seasoning salt

1 tablespoon cornstarch

Put 2¼ cups of the water and the rice in a medium saucepan and bring to a boil over high heat. Decrease the heat to low, cover, and cook until the rice is tender and the water is absorbed, about 45 minutes.

Heat the oil in a large skillet over medium heat. Add the onion and cook, stirring frequently, for 2 to 3 minutes. Add the bell pepper and garlic and cook, stirring frequently, for 5 minutes. Add the seitan, mushrooms, sherry, parsley, and seasoning salt and cook, stirring frequently, until the mushrooms begin to cook down, 5 to 7 minutes.

Put the remaining ½ cup of water and the cornstarch in a small bowl and mix well. Pour into the skillet and cook, stirring constantly, until the sauce thickens, about 3 minutes. Serve the seitan tips over the rice.

Per serving: 363 calories, 26 g protein, 6 g fat (1 g sat), 52 g carbs, 615 mg sodium, 65 mg calcium, 5 g fiber

I absolutely had to veganize chicken and dumplin's for this cookbook, since it's such a Southern tradition. This vegan version makes a hearty meal, perfect for a cool evening. We don't get many of those down here, so if you live up North, you're in luck: you can enjoy this savory, satisfying dish more often.

Seitan and Dumplin's

VEGETABLES

2 medium Yukon Gold potatoes, scrubbed and cubed

1 onion, chopped

2 to 3 carrots, peeled and sliced

1 cup frozen peas

COOKING BROTH

5 cups low-sodium vegetable broth

2 tablespoons nutritional yeast

1½ teaspoons poultry seasoning

¼ teaspoon salt

Ground pepper

DUMPLIN'S

2 cups whole wheat pastry flour, plus more for kneading

1 teaspoon baking powder

¼ teaspoon baking soda

¼ teaspoon salt

¾ cup ice water

To prepare the vegetables, put the potatoes, onion, and carrots in a large soup pot and add enough water to cover. Bring to a boil over high heat. Decrease the heat to medium, cover, and cook until the potatoes and carrots are fork-tender, 15 to 20 minutes. Remove from the heat and stir in the frozen peas. Let the peas thaw in the water for 5 minutes. Drain in a colander. Rinse the pot and return it to the stove.

To prepare the cooking broth, put the broth, nutritional yeast, poultry seasoning, salt, and as much pepper as desired in the pot and mix well. Bring to a boil over high heat. Decrease the heat to medium-low.

To make the dumplin's, put the flour, baking powder, baking soda, and salt in a large bowl and mix well. Pour in the ice water and stir to combine. Shape the dough into a ball.

Generously flour a clean work surface and put the dough on the floured surface. Sprinkle a few pinches of flour over the dough, then pat it into a square with your hands. Use a rolling pin to roll it out to a 16-inch square.

Cut the dough lengthwise into eight 2-inch strips, then cut it widthwise at 2-inch intervals to create 2-inch squares. It's okay if some of the squares don't hold their shape during the cutting process.

Bring the broth back to a boil over high heat. Add 5 to 6 dumplin' squares and stir. Repeat the process, stirring after every few dumplin's are added to the pot to prevent them from sticking together. The dumplin's should float to the surface a few seconds after they're added to the pot.

Per serving (based on 7 servings): 306 calories, 17 g protein, 1 g fat (0 g sat), 53 g carbs, 540 mg sodium, 139 mg calcium, 9 g fiber

THICKENER AND SEITAN

¼ cup water

2 tablespoons cornstarch

2 cups bite-sized chunks seitan or Seitan Chicken (page 16)

After all the dumplin's are added to the pot, stir again and return to a boil. Cook for 5 minutes, stirring once every minute to keep the dumplin's from sticking. Remove from the heat.

To prepare the thickener and finish the dish, put the water and cornstarch in a small bowl and mix well. Add the seitan and vegetables to the pot of dumplin's and stir to combine. Stir in the cornstarch mixture and cook over medium heat, stirring constantly, until the broth thickens, about 5 minutes.

In my part of the world, we pronounce the word "pecan" in a way that rhymes with "Dijon." When dreaming up this recipe, I imagined the two rhyming ingredients would make the perfect pair. Experimentation yielded delicious results: tender chunks of seitan dredged in crunchy Southern pecans and coated with a tangy maple-mustard glaze.

Dijon-Pecan Seitan with Maple-Mustard Glaze

MAKES 4 TO 6 HELPIN'S

DIJON-PECAN SEITAN

¾ cup whole wheat pastry flour

¾ teaspoon dried thyme

½ teaspoon salt

½ teaspoon ground pepper

½ cup unsweetened soy milk

½ cup Dijon mustard

2 teaspoons maple syrup

1 cup panko breadcrumbs

¾ cup finely chopped pecans

2 cups bite-sized chunks seitan or Seitan Chicken (page 16)

MAPLE-MUSTARD GLAZE

6 tablespoons nonhydrogenated vegan margarine

6 tablespoons maple syrup

6 tablespoons Dijon mustard

To prepare the seitan, preheat the oven to 375 degrees F. Spray a baking sheet with cooking spray or line it with parchment paper.

Put the flour, thyme, salt, and pepper in a small bowl and mix well. Put the soy milk, mustard, and maple syrup in another small bowl and mix well. Put the panko and pecans in a third small bowl and mix well.

Dredge a piece of the seitan in the flour mixture, coating it evenly, then dip it in the soy milk mixture. Put it in the bowl with the panko mixture, turning it and pressing firmly until evenly coated. Put the seitan on the prepared baking sheet. Repeat the process with the remaining seitan, leaving a little space between the pieces.

Bake for 30 minutes, until lightly browned and crispy, flipping the seitan halfway through the baking time.

To make the glaze, melt the margarine in a small saucepan over low heat. Stir in the maple syrup and mustard and heat, stirring occasionally, for about 2 minutes. Remove from the heat.

Put several pieces of the seitan in the saucepan and gently stir until evenly coated. Transfer to a plate with a slotted spoon. Repeat with the remaining seitan.

Per serving (based on 5 servings): 637 calories, 21 g protein, 36 g fat (5 g sat), 58 g carbs, 1,717 mg sodium, 89 mg calcium, 5 g fiber

outherners are a superstitious lot. That's why we eat black-eyed peas and cabbage (or collards for some folks) on New Year's Day. The black-eyed peas ensure prosperity in the New Year, and eating cabbage or greens brings the promise of good fortune. But don't wait until the first of January to make this healthful dish. It's delicious any day of the year.

Hoppin' John with Sausage and Brown Rice

MAKES 4 TO 6 HELPIN'S

4¼ cups water

1 cup brown rice

1 tablespoon canola oil

1 onion, chopped

1 can (14.5-ounces) **low-sodium diced tomatoes with juice**

2 cups chopped cabbage

1 cup dried black-eyed peas

½ teaspoon salt

½ teaspoon dried thyme

½ teaspoon dried marjoram

2 bay leaves

7 ounces (one-half tube) **Gimme Lean Sausage**

Hot sauce

Ground pepper

Put 2¼ cups of the water and the rice in a medium saucepan and bring to a boil over high heat. Decrease the heat to low, cover, and cook until the rice is tender and the water is absorbed, about 45 minutes.

Heat the oil in a large soup pot over medium heat. Add the onion and cook, stirring frequently, for 2 to 3 minutes. Stir in the remaining 2 cups of water and the tomatoes with their juice, cabbage, black-eyed peas, salt, thyme, marjoram, and bay leaves. Increase the heat to high and bring to a boil. Decrease the heat to medium-low, cover, and simmer, stirring occasionally, until the black-eyed peas are tender, about 45 minutes.

Slice the vegan sausage into 5 or 6 patties. Spray a medium skillet with cooking spray. Put the skillet over medium heat, add the patties, and cook until brown on the bottom, 3 to 4 minutes. Flip the patties and cook until brown on the other side, about 3 minutes. Transfer to a plate and break into bite-sized pieces with a fork.

Stir the vegan sausage into the black-eyed pea mixture and remove from the heat. Serve over the brown rice. Pass hot sauce and pepper at the table.

Per serving (based on 5 servings): 276 calories, 13 g protein, 4 g fat (0 g sat), 46 g carbs, 445 mg sodium, 68 mg calcium, 9 g fiber

I'm not sure what possessed me to put eggplant in jambalaya, but I'm glad I did. The hearty texture of sautéed eggplant combined with chewy vegan sausage makes for a perfect combination in this New Orleans classic. If you have time, try making your own Creole Steamed Sausages for this recipe.

Eggplant and Creole Sausage Jambalaya

MAKES 6 HELPIN'S

1 tablespoon canola oil

1 onion, chopped

4 cloves garlic, minced

1 green bell pepper, cut into large pieces

2 stalks celery, chopped

2 cups low-sodium vegetable broth

1 can (14.5 ounces) **low-sodium diced tomatoes with juice**

1 cup brown rice

1 to 2 tablespoons hot sauce

1½ teaspoons smoked paprika

1 teaspoon garlic powder

1 teaspoon onion powder

1 teaspoon dried oregano

1 teaspoon dried thyme

½ teaspoon salt

½ teaspoon cayenne

4 Italian or kielbasa vegan sausage links or Creole Steamed Sausages (page 19), **sliced**

1 globe eggplant, peeled and chopped

Heat the oil in large saucepan or soup pot over medium heat. Add the onion and cook, stirring frequently, for 2 to 3 minutes. Add the garlic and cook, stirring frequently, for 1 minute. Add the bell pepper and celery and cook, stirring frequently, for 5 to 7 minutes.

Add the broth, tomatoes with their juice, rice, 1 tablespoon of the hot sauce, and the paprika, garlic powder, onion powder, oregano, thyme, salt, and cayenne. Increase the heat to high and bring to a boil. Decrease the heat to medium-low, cover, and cook until the rice is tender and the liquid is absorbed, 50 to 60 minutes.

Meanwhile, spray a large skillet with cooking spray. Add the vegan sausage and cook, stirring frequently, until it begins to brown, about 5 minutes. Add the eggplant and cook, stirring frequently, until the eggplant is tender but firm, 25 to 30 minutes.

Stir the vegan sausage mixture into the rice mixture before serving.

Per serving: 230 calories, 11 g protein, 5 g fat (0 g sat), 33 g carbs, 610 mg sodium, 37 mg calcium, 37 g fiber

here I come from, we slather barbecue sauce on everything—sandwiches, nachos, spaghetti, and even pizza. Tangy barbecue tempeh stands in for chicken in this variation on a dish with a uniquely Southern spin: barbecue chicken pizza. The cheesy sauce thickens in the oven, eliminating the frustration of trying to melt store-bought vegan cheese.

BBQ Tempeh Pizza

MAKES 4 TO 8 HELPIN'S

8 ounces tempeh, sliced lengthwise into 10 to 12 strips

½ cup barbecue sauce (homemade, page 12, or store-bought)

1 (12-inch) **store-bought vegan pizza crust, unbaked**

1 cup Basic Cheesy Sauce (page 13)

1 cup baby spinach, packed

Preheat the oven to 400 degrees F.

Steam the tempeh for 10 minutes.

Spray a medium skillet with cooking spray. Crumble the tempeh into the skillet. Cook over medium heat, stirring frequently, until the tempeh is lightly browned, 3 to 5 minutes.

Pour the barbecue sauce into the skillet and stir to coat the tempeh. Cook, stirring frequently, until the tempeh absorbs most of the sauce, about 3 minutes.

Put the crust on a 12- or 14-inch pizza pan or large baking sheet and spread the cheesy sauce evenly over the top, leaving a ½-inch border. Spread the spinach over the cheese. Top with the tempeh.

Bake for 10 to 12 minutes, until the edges of the crust begin to brown and the cheesy sauce is firm.

Per serving (based on 6 servings): 262 calories, 14 g protein, 7 g fat (2 g sat), 35 g carbs, 491 mg sodium, 74 mg calcium, 5 g fiber

ornbread ain't just for crumblin' in a bowl of beans. The Southern favorite also makes a hearty crust for a veggie-packed pizza. A sturdy cast-iron skillet is highly recommended for this recipe.

Veggie Lover's Cornbread Pizza

MAKES 4 HELPIN'S

GROUND TSP BEEF

1 cup water

1 tablespoon reduced-sodium soy sauce

1 teaspoon onion powder

1 teaspoon vegan Worcestershire sauce (homemade, page 10, or store-bought)

½ cup dry TSP crumbles (see page 5)

PIZZA SAUCE

1 teaspoon extra-virgin olive oil

2 cloves garlic, minced

1 can (8 ounces) **no-salt-added tomato sauce**

½ teaspoon dried oregano

½ teaspoon dried basil

VEGETABLES

1 tablespoon canola oil

½ cup chopped Vidalia onion

1 cup sliced summer squash, in thin half-moons

½ red bell pepper, cut into thin strips

To make the ground TSP beef, put the water, soy sauce, onion powder, and Worcestershire sauce in a small saucepan and mix well. Bring to a boil over high heat. Add the TSP crumbles. Decrease the heat to medium-low, cover, and cook, stirring occasionally, until most of the liquid is absorbed, about 20 minutes. Drain in a fine-mesh sieve.

To make the pizza sauce, heat the oil in a small saucepan over medium heat. Add the garlic and cook, stirring frequently, for 1 minute. Add the tomato sauce, oregano, and basil, decrease the heat to medium-low, and simmer, stirring occasionally, for 10 minutes.

To prepare the vegetables, heat the oil in a large skillet over medium heat. Add the onion and cook, stirring frequently, for 2 to 3 minutes. Add the squash and bell pepper and cook, stirring frequently, until the vegetables are slightly tender, 5 to 7 minutes. Add the kale and cook, stirring frequently, until the kale is wilted and the vegetables are tender, 8 to 12 minutes. Stir in the greens seasoning and hot sauce to taste.

To make the cornbread crust, preheat the oven to 400 degrees F. Spray a 10-inch cast-iron skillet or a 10-inch deep-dish pizza pan with cooking spray.

Put the cornmeal, flour, sugar, baking powder, baking soda, and salt in a large bowl and mix well.

Put the water and egg replacer in a small bowl and whisk until the egg replacer is dissolved and the mixture is foamy. Stir in the soy milk, vinegar, and oil. Pour into the cornmeal mixture and stir until just combined.

Per serving: 352 calories, 22 g protein, 9 g fat (1 g sat), 48 g carbs, 1,006 mg sodium, 248 mg calcium, 8 g fiber

2 cups chopped kale, packed

½ teaspoon greens seasoning or
   other seasoning salt (see note),
   plus more if desired

Hot sauce

CORNBREAD CRUST

½ cup yellow cornmeal

½ cup whole wheat pastry flour

1 tablespoon sugar

1 teaspoon baking powder

½ teaspoon baking soda

¼ teaspoon salt

2 tablespoons warm water

1½ teaspoons Ener-G egg replacer

½ cup unsweetened soy milk

1½ teaspoons cider vinegar

1½ teaspoons canola oil

To assemble and bake the pizza, spread the cornmeal mixture in the prepared skillet. Top with ½ to ¾ cup of the pizza sauce (reserve any leftovers to use in another dish), leaving a ½-inch border. Spread the TSP ground beef over the pizza sauce, then top with as much of the veggie mixture as will fit (reserve any leftovers to serve as a side dish at another meal). It's okay if the vegetables are piled high.

Bake for 30 minutes, until the edges of the crust are browned. Top with more hot sauce and greens seasoning if desired.

NOTE: Greens seasoning is a blend of salt and sugar made especially for adding a special sweet 'n' savory kick to cooked greens. It's available at most well-stocked grocery stores, but if you can't find it, substitute your favorite seasoning salt.

FOR THE POTLUCK

CASSEROLES AND SAVORY PIES

I'll confess that I haven't been to a church potluck in years, but I still remember the dairy-laden retro casseroles at Me-Maw's tiny Southern Baptist church. Folks would pile dishes on folding tables in the church gym and load their plates with a variety of cheesy, creamy casseroles.

This chapter features simple one-dish oven-baked recipes that warm the kitchen and would surely impress the parishioners at Me-Maw's place of worship. Just don't tell 'em that the white stuff is tofu! Serve these dairy-free versions of traditional casseroles at your next potluck, or make 'em for a main course at home. Dishes like Creamy Tofu Chicken Pasta Bake (page 114), Hash Brown Casserole (page 110), and Seitan and Root Veggie Potpie (page 115) are sure bets, and definitely try my mama's famous vegan cornbread dressin' (page 112) at your next holiday meal.

O ne of my testers served this veganized version of my granny's beloved squash casserole to her squash-hating husband. Guess what? He loved it! That's no wonder, since this creamy dish, which contains brown rice, is reminiscent of a comforting risotto. The baking time is on the long side, so plan ahead. Despite the long cooking time, it sure beats all of that tiresome stirring needed for risotto.

Creamy Squash Casserole

1 cup low-sodium vegetable broth

¼ cup water

2 tablespoons cornstarch

1 tablespoon nonhydrogenated vegan margarine

1 onion, diced

3 medium summer squash, thinly sliced

2 cups unsweetened soy milk

1 cup brown rice

½ teaspoon salt

Ground pepper

Preheat the oven to 375 degrees F. Spray a 4-quart casserole dish with cooking spray.

Bring the broth to a boil in a small saucepan over high heat. Put the water and cornstarch in a small bowl and mix well. Pour into the broth and whisk until thoroughly blended. Decrease the heat to medium and cook, stirring constantly with the whisk, until thick and creamy, 5 to 7 minutes. Remove from the heat.

Melt the margarine in a small skillet over medium heat. Add the onion and cook, stirring frequently, until tender, 4 to 5 minutes. Transfer to the prepared casserole dish and add the broth mixture, squash, soy milk, rice, salt, and as much pepper as desired. Mix well, then spread the mixture in an even layer.

Cover and bake for about 90 minutes, stirring every 30 minutes and then covering again, until the rice is tender.

Per serving (based on 7 servings): 180 calories, 7 g protein, 4 g fat (1 g sat), 30 g carbs, 222 mg sodium, 42 mg calcium, 3 g fiber

y granny has numerous versions of corn casserole in her repertoire, and when I asked for the recipe of my childhood favorite, she couldn't remember which one I'd liked so much. I seem to recall a Cheddar-covered corn casserole, but she suggested I try veganizing this cream cheese–laden version. Though I don't remember eating this as a kid, I think I like it even better than the casserole I remember.

Granny's Corn Casserole

MAKES 6 HELPIN'S

8 ounces vegan cream cheese, at room temperature (see note)

2 tablespoons nonhydrogenated vegan margarine, at room temperature

2 cups frozen corn kernels

1 jar (2 ounces) **sliced pimientos, drained**

1 can (4 ounces) **diced green chiles, drained**

¼ teaspoon salt

Ground pepper

Paprika, for garnish

Preheat the oven to 400 degrees F. Spray a 1½-quart casserole dish with cooking spray.

Put the vegan cream cheese and margarine in a large bowl and stir until creamy and well combined. Stir in the corn, pimientos, chiles, salt, and as much pepper as desired.

Transfer to the prepared casserole dish and spread in an even layer. Dust the top with paprika.

Bake uncovered for 35 minutes, until golden brown.

NOTE: For vegan cream cheese, I recommend Tofutti brand Better Than Cream Cheese or Galaxy Nutritional Foods Vegan Cream Cheese.

Per serving: 118 calories, 2 g protein, 6 g fat (2 g sat), 15 g carbs, 161 mg sodium, 11 mg calcium, 2 g fiber

This comfort-food casserole has been an essential side dish at family holiday gatherings as far back as I can remember. My mom's nonvegan version was actually one of the last dairy-laden dishes I gorged on before going vegan the day after Thanksgiving in 2004. In fact, that was the one dish that made me think twice before giving up dairy cheese. But thanks to my vegan cream of mushroom soup and shredded vegan Cheddar, removing the dairy is a cinch. Now my mom makes the vegan version of this casserole every Thanksgiving.

Hash Brown Casserole

MAKES 8 TO 10 HELPIN'S

3 tablespoons nonhydrogenated vegan margarine

1 onion, diced

1 large bag (1 pound, 14 ounces) frozen hash browns, thawed

2 cups creamy vegan mushroom soup (homemade, page 68, or store-bought)

2 cups shredded vegan Cheddar cheese

1½ cups vegan sour cream

½ teaspoon salt

½ teaspoon ground pepper

2 cups crushed corn flakes

Preheat the oven to 350 degrees F. Spray a 13 x 9-inch baking pan with cooking spray.

Melt 2 tablespoons of the margarine in a small skillet over medium heat. Add the onion and cook, stirring frequently, until the onion is very tender, 5 to 7 minutes.

Put the hash browns in the prepared pan. Add the onion, mushroom soup, vegan cheese, vegan sour cream, salt, and pepper and stir until well combined. Spread the mixture in an even layer.

Melt the remaining tablespoon of margarine in a small saucepan over medium heat. Put the corn flakes in a medium bowl and pour the margarine evenly over the top. Stir gently to evenly coat the corn flakes. Sprinkle evenly over the hash brown mixture.

Bake uncovered for 45 minutes, until golden brown.

Per serving (based on 9 servings): 574 calories, 13 g protein, 31 g fat (11 g sat), 57 g carbs, 870 mg sodium, 36 mg calcium, 4 g fiber

A t every Southern family reunion, you can bet your bottom dollar that one of the aunts or cousins brings a piping-hot casserole of broccoli, rice, and cheese. But what's in that homemade concoction? Probably a processed cheese product and nutritionally void white rice. Here's a more healthful version made with nutritional yeast and brown rice.

Cheesy Broccoli-Rice Casserole

Advance preparation required

1 head broccoli

2 tablespoons nonhydrogenated vegan margarine

½ onion, diced

1 tablespoon reduced-sodium soy sauce

2 cups cooked brown rice (see note)

1 cup creamy vegan mushroom soup (homemade, page 68, or store-bought)

Salt

Ground pepper

1 cup Basic Cheesy Sauce (page 13)

½ cup dry whole wheat breadcrumbs

Preheat the oven to 350 degrees F. Spray a 2½-quart casserole dish with cooking spray.

Cut the stems off the broccoli and trim away the tough end. Peel the stems with a vegetable peeler, then chop them into bite-sized pieces. Cut the broccoli tops into bite-sized florets.

Melt the margarine in a large skillet over medium heat. Add the onion and cook, stirring frequently, for 2 to 3 minutes. Add the broccoli and soy sauce and stir until the broccoli is evenly coated. Cook, stirring frequently, until the broccoli just begins to soften, 8 to 10 minutes. Transfer to a large bowl.

Add the rice and mushroom soup and mix well. Season with salt and pepper to taste. Transfer the mixture to the prepared casserole dish and spread it in an even layer. Drizzle the cheesy sauce evenly over the mixture, then sprinkle the breadcrumbs evenly over the top.

Bake uncovered for 30 minutes, then place under the broiler for 2 to 3 minutes, until the breadcrumbs are golden brown.

NOTE: Either leftover or freshly cooked brown rice can be used in this recipe. To make about 3 cups of cooked brown rice, put 1 cup of brown rice and 2¼ cups of water in a medium saucepan. Bring to a boil over high heat. Decrease the heat to low, cover, and cook until the rice is tender and the water is absorbed, about 45 minutes. Save the leftovers for use in another meal.

Per serving (based on 7 servings): 233 calories, 9 g protein, 8 g fat (2 g sat), 31 g carbs, 373 mg sodium, 65 mg calcium, 3 g fiber

My mama is famous for her cornbread dressin'. Folks have tried to re-create it, but Mama must have cast some spell to prevent anyone from outdoing her dressin'. Even when other people use my mama's recipe, they can't even come close to the dressin' she makes. When I went vegan in 2004, Mama came up with an equally tasty vegan version that she makes every Thanksgiving and Christmas. She passed her recipe on to me, and now I'm sharing it with y'all.

Mama's Vegan Cornbread Dressin'

MAKES 8 TO 12 HELPIN'S

CORNBREAD

2 cups unsweetened soy milk

2 tablespoons cider vinegar

2 cups yellow cornmeal

2 cups whole wheat pastry flour

¼ cup sugar

1 tablespoon plus 1 teaspoon
baking powder

2 teaspoons baking soda

1 teaspoon salt

½ cup warm water

2 tablespoons Ener-G egg replacer

2 tablespoons canola oil

DRESSIN'

¼ cup nonhydrogenated vegan
margarine

1 onion, chopped

2 slices whole wheat or whole-grain
bread, toasted

4 cups low-sodium vegetable broth

2 cups creamy vegan celery soup
(homemade, page 69, or
store-bought)

2½ teaspoons rubbed sage

1 teaspoon salt

Ground pepper

To make the cornbread, preheat the oven to 400 degrees F. Spray two 9-inch round baking pans with cooking spray.

Put the soy milk and vinegar in a small bowl and stir well. Set aside until the soy milk curdles and thickens, about 2 minutes.

Put the cornmeal, flour, sugar, baking powder, baking soda, and salt in a large bowl and mix well.

Put the water and egg replacer in a medium bowl and whisk until the egg replacer is dissolved and the mixture is foamy. Stir in the soy milk mixture and oil. Pour into the cornmeal mixture and stir until just combined. Don't overmix.

Spread the batter in the prepared pans, dividing it evenly between them. Bake for 30 minutes, until a toothpick inserted in the middle comes out clean. Remove from the oven and turn the oven temperature down to 350 degrees F.

To make the dressin', spray a 13 x 9-inch casserole dish with cooking spray.

Melt the margarine in a small skillet over medium heat. Add the onion and cook, stirring frequently, until tender, 4 to 5 minutes.

Crumble the cornbread into the casserole dish. Tear the toast into small chunks and add them to the casserole dish. Add the onion and any melted margarine left in the skillet, along with the broth, celery soup, sage, salt, and as much pepper as desired. Mix well, then spread the mixture in an even layer.

Bake uncovered for 40 minutes, until firm and lightly browned.

Per serving (based on 10 servings): 343 calories, 8 g protein, 10 g fat (2 g sat), 53 g carbs, 1,040 mg sodium, 194 mg calcium, 7 g fiber

I have a distant memory of my granny making these tangy beer beans when I was a kid. Unfortunately, she doesn't remember ever making beer beans, and no one else in my family remembers it either. They all think I dreamed up this recipe. Maybe I did, but when I re-created the recipe from memory (or my dreams), the boozy concoction tasted just like Granny's beer beans from my childhood (or at least the childhood of my dreams).

Boozy Baked Beans

1 tablespoon canola oil

1 small onion, chopped

2 cloves garlic, minced

2 cans (14 to 16 ounces each) **cannellini beans, drained and rinsed**

1 tablespoon water

1 tablespoon cornstarch

¾ cup dark vegan beer (see note)

¼ cup ketchup

1 tablespoon molasses

½ teaspoon salt

½ teaspoon liquid smoke

¼ teaspoon dry mustard

Ground pepper

Preheat the oven to 400 degrees F. Spray a 2½-quart casserole dish with cooking spray.

Heat the oil in a small skillet over medium heat. Add the onion and cook, stirring frequently, until tender, 4 to 5 minutes. Add the garlic and cook, stirring frequently, for 1 minute.

Put the beans in the prepared casserole dish. Put the water and cornstarch in a small bowl and mix well. Add to the beans along with the onion, beer, ketchup, molasses, salt, liquid smoke, mustard, and as much pepper as desired. Mix well, then spread the mixture in an even layer.

Cover and bake for 45 minutes. Uncover and bake for about 15 minutes longer, until the beans are browned around the edges.

NOTE: You can use any type of vegan beer for this recipe, but I recommend using a high-quality dark microbrew, like a stout, porter, or nut brown ale. For a comprehensive list of vegan beers, go to barnivore.com.

Per serving (based on 5 servings): 186 calories, 8 g protein, 3 g fat (0 g sat), 22 g carbs, 381 mg sodium, 100 mg calcium, 9 g fiber

Every Southern cook has a standard church potluck dish, even those who don't attend church. While this one's never seen the inside of a chapel, I'm certain it would go over well with the church folk.

Creamy Tofu Chicken Pasta Bake

Advance preparation required

MAKES 6 HELPIN'S

6 ounces quinoa macaroni or whole wheat macaroni

1 cup low-sodium vegetable broth

1 onion, chopped

1 green bell pepper, chopped

2 stalks celery, diced

1 can (14.5 ounces) **low-sodium diced tomatoes, drained**

1 cup creamy vegan mushroom soup (homemade, page 68, or store-bought)

1 pound Tofu Chicken (page 15)**, with the tofu cut into bite-sized cubes and marinated but not baked**

Salt

Ground pepper

¼ cup nutritional yeast

Preheat the oven to 400 degrees F. Spray a 2½-quart casserole dish with cooking spray.

Bring a large pot of salted water to a boil over high heat. Stir in the macaroni. Decrease the heat to medium-low and cook, stirring occasionally, until tender but firm. Drain well.

Meanwhile, put the broth, onion, bell pepper, and celery in a large saucepan and bring to a boil over medium-high heat. Decrease the heat to medium, cover, and cook, stirring occasionally, until the vegetables are tender, about 8 minutes. Stir in the tomatoes and mushroom soup. Cook, stirring frequently, for about 7 minutes. Remove from the heat.

Drain the tofu chicken. Add the tofu chicken and macaroni to the saucepan and stir gently until thoroughly combined. Season with salt and pepper to taste.

Transfer the mixture to the prepared casserole dish and spread it in an even layer. Scatter the nutritional yeast evenly over the top. Cover and bake for 30 minutes, until bubbly.

Per serving: 257 calories, 16 g protein, 6 g fat (1 g sat), 35 g carbs, 349 mg sodium, 164 mg calcium, 5 g fiber

I love all kinds of pie, but I tend to choose savory dishes over sweet ones. I'll take my flaky pie crust stuffed with veggies and gravy over a dessert pie any day. This potpie features tender seitan chunks and hearty root vegetables, making it the perfect supper for an autumn evening.

Seitan and Root Veggie Potpie

MAKES 6 HELPIN'S

2 **Whole Wheat Pie Crusts** (page 146)

1 tablespoon canola oil

1 cup chopped white onion

2 cups low-sodium vegetable broth

1 cup peeled and diced white potato

1 cup peeled and diced sweet potato

1 cup peeled and diced turnip

1 carrot, peeled and sliced

½ teaspoon salt

½ teaspoon dried thyme

½ teaspoon dried marjoram

½ teaspoon Greek seasoning salt or other seasoning salt

Ground pepper

¼ cup water

2 tablespoons cornstarch

2 cups bite-sized chunks seitan or **Seitan Chicken** (page 16)

Preheat the oven to 350 degrees F.

Line a 9-inch pie pan with one pie crust and set the other crust aside for topping the potpie.

Heat the oil in a large saucepan over medium heat. Add the onion and cook, stirring frequently, for 2 to 3 minutes. Add the broth, white potato, sweet potato, turnip, carrot, salt, thyme, marjoram, seasoning salt, and as much pepper as desired and mix well. Increase the heat to high and bring to a boil. Decrease the heat to medium, cover, and simmer, stirring occasionally, until the vegetables are tender, about 15 minutes.

Put the water and cornstarch in a small bowl and mix well. Pour into the saucepan and cook, stirring constantly, until the mixture thickens, 3 to 5 minutes. Remove from the heat and stir in the seitan.

Scoop the mixture into the pie crust using a slotted spoon (discard the remaining gravy). Cover the potpie with the top crust and trim away any dough that hangs over the edge of the pan. Seal the edges by crimping the two layers of dough together with a fork. Pierce the top crust a few times with the tines of the fork.

Bake for 35 minutes, until the edges of the crust start to brown.

Per serving: 588 calories, 19 g protein, 28 g fat (12 g sat), 64 g carbs, 742 mg sodium, 106 mg calcium, 11 g fiber

his recipe is adapted from a dish my mom used to make called Hungry Jack Casserole. She used Hungry Jack brand canned biscuits, ground beef, Cheddar cheese, and pork 'n' beans, which is obviously a long way from being vegan. In this version, I've subbed TSP for the ground beef and white beans seasoned with tangy barbecue sauce for the pork 'n' beans. Although some canned biscuits are vegan, most are loaded with trans fats, so this recipe uses homemade biscuit dough for a more healthful casserole.

Hungry Jill Casserole

BISCUIT TOPPING

½ cup unsweetened soy milk

1 teaspoon cider vinegar

1¼ cups whole wheat pastry flour, plus more for sprinkling

1½ teaspoons baking powder

¼ teaspoon salt

¼ teaspoon baking soda

1½ tablespoons nonhydrogenated vegetable shortening

1 tablespoon nonhydrogenated vegan margarine

To make the biscuit topping, put the soy milk and vinegar in a small bowl and stir well. Set aside until the soy milk curdles and thickens, about 2 minutes.

Sift the flour, baking powder, salt, and baking soda together into a large bowl and mix well. Add the shortening and margarine and cut them in with a pastry blender or your hands until the texture resembles coarse crumbs.

Pour in the soy milk mixture and mix well. You'll need to dig in with your hands and lightly knead the mixture in the bowl to make sure all the ingredients are well combined. Don't overmix, or the biscuits won't be light and fluffy. Sprinkle a couple of generous pinches of flour over the top of the dough while it's still in the bowl, but don't mix it in.

Transfer the dough to a liberally floured work surface (a generous amount of flour is needed because the dough tends to be a little sticky). Lightly roll out or pat down the dough until it's about ¾ inch thick.

The aim is to cut 6 biscuits from the dough. Start by cutting as many biscuits as you can with a 2½-inch biscuit cutter. Press the cutter into the dough and then lift it straight up. Don't twist the cutter, or the baked biscuits will be flat. Carefully transfer the cut biscuits to a plate.

Gather up the remaining bits of dough. Roll or pat down until ¾ inch thick and cut the remaining biscuits. Cut each biscuit in half crosswise.

Per serving (based on 7 servings): 338 calories, 20 g protein, 10 g fat (2 g sat), 41 g carbs, 990 mg sodium, 193 mg calcium, 9 g fiber

FILLING

2 teaspoons canola oil

½ cup chopped onion

2 cans (14 to 16 ounces each) **Great Northern beans, drained and rinsed**

1 cup Ground TSP Beef (page 18)

¾ cup barbecue sauce (homemade, page 12, or store-bought)

¼ cup water

3 tablespoons nutritional yeast

¼ teaspoon garlic powder

¼ teaspoon ground cumin

Salt

1 cup shredded vegan Cheddar cheese

To make the filling, heat the oil in a small skillet over medium heat. Add the onion and cook, stirring frequently, for 4 to 5 minutes. Transfer to a large bowl. Add the beans, ground TSP beef, barbecue sauce, water, nutritional yeast, garlic powder, and cumin and mix well. Season with salt to taste.

To assemble and bake the casserole, preheat the oven to 375 degrees F. Spray a 2½-quart casserole dish with cooking spray. Pour the filling mixture into the prepared casserole dish. Put the biscuit halves along the edges of the casserole dish cut-side down (with the rounded edge facing up). If you run out of space, arrange the remaining biscuit halves cut-side down in the center of the casserole. Scatter the vegan cheese over the exposed filling between the biscuits, making sure not to cover the biscuits.

Bake uncovered for about 30 minutes, until the biscuits are golden.

I f you plan on making homemade tamales, you'd better have a whole day set aside. Although the laborious task yields delicious results, who has time for all that? I created this Hot Tamale Pie as an easy shortcut for busy folks with a taste for tamales.

Hot Tamale Pie

¾ cup yellow cornmeal

½ cup cold water

3 cups low-sodium vegetable broth

½ teaspoon seasoning salt

1 tablespoon canola oil

1 yellow onion, chopped

1 jalapeño chile, minced

2 cloves garlic, minced

1 green bell pepper, chopped

1 can (14.5 ounces) low-sodium diced tomatoes, drained

1 can (14 to 16 ounces) pinto beans, drained and rinsed

1 cup frozen corn kernels, thawed

1 tablespoon nutritional yeast

1 tablespoon chili powder

1 teaspoon ground cumin

Preheat the oven to 350 degrees F. Spray a 10-inch pie pan with cooking spray.

Put the cornmeal and water in a medium saucepan and mix well, then whisk in the broth. Bring to a simmer over medium-high heat. At the first sign of bubbling, decrease the heat to low, cover, and cook until thick, 10 to 15 minutes, stirring frequently to prevent lumps. Stir in ¼ teaspoon of the seasoning salt.

Heat the oil in a large saucepan or deep skillet over medium heat. Add the onion and cook, stirring frequently, for 2 to 3 minutes. Add the chile and garlic and cook, stirring frequently, for 1 minute. Add the bell pepper and cook, stirring frequently, until it begins to soften, 5 to 7 minutes.

Stir in the tomatoes, beans, corn, nutritional yeast, chili powder, cumin, and the remaining ¼ teaspoon of seasoning salt. Cook, stirring occasionally, for 10 minutes.

Put half of the cornmeal mixture in the prepared pie pan and spread it evenly over the bottom and along the sides. Put about 4 cups of the bean mixture in the pan (reserve any leftovers to use as a topping for nachos or a filling for burritos). Spread the remaining cornmeal mixture evenly over the bean mixture. It's okay if some of the bean mixture is visible around the edges.

Bake for about 30 minutes, until the top is slightly crusty and browned.

Per serving (based on 5 servings): 240 calories, 9 g protein, 4 g fat (0 g sat), 37 g carbs, 228 mg sodium, 62 mg calcium, 10 g fiber

ALL THE FIXIN'S

SAVORY SIDES

From stewed okra to dirty rice, no down-home supper is complete without a few veggie- or grain-based side dishes. In this chapter you'll find my treasured Mess o' Greens with Turnips recipe (page 120), which boasts all the smoky flavor of slow-cooked greens, but without the bacon fat. Other great choices to accompany your next main course include Spicy Jalapeño Hominy (page 121), Fried Green Tomatoes (page 129), or Nutty Mushroom Quinoa (page 133). Oh, and please don't fear the Fried Cucumbers (page 131). You haven't had a cucumber until you've had one sliced, coated in batter, fried, and served with a side of Country Buttermilk Ranch Dressing (page 9).

In recent years, some folks have tried to "healthify" traditional Southern slow-cooked collard greens by shortening the cooking time to about twenty minutes. But where I come from, cooking collards for anything less than forty minutes is blasphemy. The secret to a perfect pot of greens is patience. Also, don't throw out the cooking liquid when the greens are done. In the South we call that pot likker, and it's perfect for dippin' cornbread into or adding to soups and stews.

Mess o' Greens with Turnips

MAKES 2 TO 4 HELPIN'S

1 cup low-sodium vegetable broth

1 tablespoon sugar

1 tablespoon extra-virgin olive oil

1 teaspoon liquid smoke

½ teaspoon salt

¼ teaspoon ground pepper

1 bunch collard, turnip, or mustard greens, stemmed and torn into small pieces

2 small turnips, peeled and diced

Hot sauce

Put the broth, sugar, oil, liquid smoke, salt, and pepper in a large soup pot and mix well. Add the greens and turnips. Cover and cook over medium heat, stirring occasionally, until the greens wilt. Decrease the heat to medium-low, cover, and simmer, stirring occasionally, until the greens lose their bitter flavor and the turnips are very tender, 35 to 40 minutes. Season with hot sauce to taste.

Per serving (based on 3 servings): 92 calories, 2 g protein, 5 g fat (1 g sat), 8 g carbs, 424 mg sodium, 102 mg calcium, 4 g fiber

o many folks write off Brussels sprouts after one bad childhood experience. But I promise they taste much better as your taste buds grow more sophisticated. Still skeptical? Since everything tastes better caramelized, this recipe is perfect for reintroducing your palate to these tiny cabbages.

Caramelized Brussels Sprouts with Pecans

MAKES 2 TO 4 HELPIN'S

1 pound Brussels sprouts

1 tablespoon canola oil

⅓ cup chopped pecans

1 tablespoon sugar

2 cloves garlic, minced

¼ teaspoon crushed red pepper flakes

¼ teaspoon salt

Trim and discard the stem ends from the Brussels sprouts. Discard any scraggly outer leaves. Cut the Brussels sprouts in half and steam them for 8 minutes.

Fill a large bowl with water and about 1 cup of ice cubes. After the Brussels sprouts have steamed for 8 minutes, immediately transfer them to the ice water to stop the cooking. Leave them in the cold water for about 3 minutes, then drain well.

Heat the oil in a large, heavy skillet over medium-high heat. Add the Brussels sprouts, placing them flat-side down. Cook without stirring until the flat sides are browned, 10 to 12 minutes.

Decrease the heat to medium and stir in the pecans, sugar, garlic, red pepper flakes, and salt. Cook, stirring occasionally, until the pecans are toasted and the Brussels sprouts are tender, 4 to 5 minutes.

Per serving (based on 3 servings): 211 calories, 6 g protein, 14 g fat (1 g sat), 13 g carbs, 216 mg sodium, 76 mg calcium, 7 g fiber

y mom calls this fried cabbage, but it's actually sautéed. In the South, we'll call anything fried if we can get away with it. But so as not to be deceiving, I renamed my mom's recipe for what it really is—chopped cabbage and onions cooked long and slow until caramelized and crispy.

Caramelized Cabbage and Onion

MAKES 4 HELPIN'S

1 tablespoon canola oil

4 cups chopped cabbage

1 onion, chopped

2 tablespoons sugar

2 tablespoons water

Salt

Ground pepper

Heat the oil in a large, heavy skillet over medium-high heat. Add the cabbage and onion and stir to coat with the oil. The pan may be very full, making it difficult to stir at first, but the cabbage will cook down.

Sprinkle in the sugar and stir until the vegetables are evenly coated. Add the water and cook without stirring until the cabbage begins to brown, about 15 minutes. If the cabbage isn't browning after 15 minutes, stir, then cook without stirring until the cabbage is golden brown, about 10 minutes longer. If the cabbage still isn't brown after 10 minutes, stir again, then cook without stirring until the cabbage is golden brown, about 10 minutes longer. Season with salt and pepper to taste.

Per serving: 287 calories, 4 g protein, 14 g fat (1 g sat), 33 g carbs, 50 mg sodium, 113 mg calcium, 7 g fiber

y mom and plenty of other Southern cooks call this homey side dish "fried corn." But it's not actually fried at all. Instead, the sweet corn kernels are boiled and thickened with a creamy soy milk mixture. The "fried" part likely has something to do with the crispy brown bits that form when the mixture thickens and the caramelized corn starts sticking to the pan.

Un-fried Corn

MAKES 5 TO 6 HELPIN'S

3 cups frozen corn kernels, thawed

1 cup unsweetened soy milk

2 tablespoons nonhydrogenated
    vegan margarine

1½ teaspoons sugar

½ teaspoon salt

1 tablespoon whole wheat pastry flour

Ground pepper

Put the corn, soy milk, margarine, sugar, and salt in a large saucepan over medium-high heat and mix well. Bring to a boil, then decrease the heat to medium-low, cover, and simmer for 10 minutes.

Sprinkle the flour over the mixture and stir it in. Cook uncovered, stirring occasionally, for 20 minutes, until most of the liquid has cooked off and the corn is just beginning to brown and stick to the pan. Season with pepper to taste.

Per serving (based on 5.5 servings): 156 calories, 5 g protein, 5 g fat (1 g sat), 24 g carbs, 257 mg sodium, 20 mg calcium, 3 g fiber

hated hominy when I was a little girl, but thankfully our taste buds get more adventurous as we age. I owe my dear friend Wes, a talented old-school country cook, for reintroducing me to this comforting side dish when I was in my midtwenties. I based this recipe on his heavily peppered version and then added jalapeño for a spicy kick.

Spicy Jalapeño Hominy

MAKES 4 HELPIN'S

1 tablespoon nonhydrogenated vegan margarine

1 jalapeño chile, minced

1 can (about 15 ounces) **white hominy, drained**

1 can (about 15 ounces) **golden hominy, drained**

¾ teaspoon ground pepper

Salt

Melt the margarine in a large skillet over medium heat. Add the chile and cook, stirring frequently, for 2 to 3 minutes. Stir in the hominy and pepper. Increase the heat to medium-high and cook, stirring frequently, until the hominy is heated through, 10 to 12 minutes. Season with salt to taste.

NOTE: Hominy is made from dried corn kernels soaked in a lye solution. The soaking forces the hull and germ to split, allowing the inner kernel to be easily removed. This process makes the corn more digestible and also converts some of the niacin into a form that's more usable by the body. Hominy can be found with other canned vegetables or in the Mexican or Latin American sections at most supermarkets.

Per serving: 84 calories, 1 g protein, 3 g fat (1 g sat), 10 g carbs, 198 mg sodium, 8 mg calcium, 2 g fiber

ost soul food restaurants serve some version of this quintessential Southern dish: smoky, slow-cooked okra and juicy tomatoes with just a touch of sweetness. Of course, the vegan version doesn't include bacon, which is traditional; it gets a similar flavor from liquid smoke, an essential in every vegan pantry.

Smoky Stewed Okra and Tomatoes

See photo facing page 150.

MAKES 4 HELPIN'S

1 tablespoon canola oil

1 onion, chopped

2 cloves garlic, minced

1 can (28 ounces) **low-sodium diced tomatoes with juice**

2 teaspoons agave nectar

½ teaspoon liquid smoke

½ teaspoon salt

3 cups sliced fresh okra

Hot sauce

Ground pepper

Heat the oil in a medium saucepan over medium-high heat. Add the onion and cook, stirring frequently, for 2 to 3 minutes. Add the garlic and cook, stirring frequently, for 1 minute.

Stir in the tomatoes and their juice and the agave nectar, liquid smoke, and salt. Increase the heat to high and bring to a boil. Decrease the heat to medium-low, cover, and simmer for 10 minutes.

Stir in the okra. Increase the heat to high and bring to a boil. Decrease the heat to medium-low, partially cover, and simmer until the okra is tender but not falling apart, 15 to 20 minutes. Season with hot sauce and pepper to taste.

Per serving: 113 calories, 4 g protein, 4 g fat (0 g sat), 15 g carbs, 291 mg sodium, 103 mg calcium, 7 g fiber

hoever thought of baking a potato twice? It seems like a crazy idea, but the result is a creamy, flavorful spud that far surpasses its once-baked counterpart. These taters are packed with savory leeks and garlic, cheesy nutritional yeast, and dried dill. You can even eat the skins for a fiber-packed nutritional punch!

Cheesy Twice-Baked Taters with Leeks and Dill

See photo facing page 150.

MAKES 2 TO 4 HELPIN'S

2 large baking potatoes, scrubbed

2 tablespoons nonhydrogenated vegan margarine

2 tablespoons thinly sliced leek, white part only

2 cloves garlic, minced

2 to 4 tablespoons unsweetened soy milk

1 tablespoon nutritional yeast

½ teaspoon salt

¼ teaspoon dried dill weed

Ground pepper

Shredded vegan Cheddar cheese (optional)

Chopped fresh chives, for garnish

Preheat the oven to 400 degrees F.

Wrap the potatoes in aluminum foil and put them on a baking sheet or directly on the oven rack. Bake for about 1 hour, until fork-tender. Cut each potato in half and let cool slightly. Leave the oven on.

Melt the margarine in a small skillet over medium heat. Add the leek and cook, stirring frequently, for 3 minutes. Add the garlic and cook, stirring frequently, for 1 minute.

Carefully scoop the potato flesh into a medium bowl, being sure to leave the potato skins completely intact and leaving a bit of potato flesh lining the skin. Don't worry if there are a few small tears in the skins. They don't have to look perfect. Set the skins aside.

Mash the potato flesh with a potato masher or a fork. Add the leek mixture, 2 tablespoons of the soy milk, and the nutritional yeast, salt, and dill weed and mix well. The mixture should be creamy but firm; if it seems dry, stir in 1 to 2 more tablespoons of soy milk. Season with pepper to taste.

Spoon the mashed potatoes into the skins, dividing them evenly. Top with the vegan cheese if desired. Garnish with chives.

Put the stuffed potatoes on a baking sheet and bake for 20 minutes, until heated through. If using the optional vegan cheese, put a deep baking pan upside down over the top of the potatoes for the last 5 minutes of baking; this will help the vegan cheese melt.

Per serving (based on 3 servings): 272 calories, 6 g protein, 8 g fat (2 g sat), 41 g carbs, 463 mg sodium, 42 mg calcium, 5 g fiber

This creamy side dish is sugary enough to satisfy your sweet tooth but savory enough to serve alongside a hearty entrée.

Mashed Sweet Taters

2 pounds sweet potatoes (about 2 large or 3 medium)**, peeled and cubed**

⅓ cup unsweetened soy milk, plus more if desired

2 tablespoons nonhydrogenated vegan margarine

2 teaspoons maple syrup

½ teaspoon salt

¼ teaspoon ground nutmeg

Ground pepper

Put the sweet potatoes in a large pot and add water to cover. Bring to a boil over high heat. Decrease the heat to medium-low, cover, and cook until fork-tender, about 20 minutes.

Drain and return to the pot or transfer to a large bowl. Add the soy milk, margarine, maple syrup, salt, and nutmeg. Mash with a potato masher or a fork, stirring as you go to make sure all the ingredients are evenly distributed. If the sweet potatoes aren't creamy enough for your liking, add more soy milk, 1 tablespoon at a time, to reach the desired consistency. Season with pepper to taste.

Per serving (based on 5 servings): 194 calories, 3 g protein, 5 g fat (1 g sat), 30 g carbs, 317 mg sodium, 56 mg calcium, 5 g fiber

I grew up wholeheartedly believing that I hated sweet potatoes. Why? Because my mom told me they were gross, and I mistakenly took her word for it. Turns out Mama had only tried sweet potatoes as candied yams, loaded with sugar and marshmallows. She didn't realize that sweet taters could be cooked up savory and spicy too. The tuber's natural sweetness balances perfectly with the salt and curry powder in this recipe. My mom is no longer a sweet tater hater thanks to her discovery of sweet potato fries.

Curried Sweet Tater Fries

MAKES 2 TO 4 HELPIN'S

2 medium sweet potatoes, peeled

1 tablespoon curry powder

1 tablespoon paprika

1 teaspoon ground cumin

½ teaspoon salt

½ teaspoon cayenne

¼ teaspoon ground pepper, plus more if desired

3 cups canola oil, for frying

Cut the potatoes into French fry shapes about ¼ inch thick.

Put the curry powder, paprika, cumin, salt, cayenne, and pepper in a large bowl and mix well. Set aside.

Line a plate with several layers of paper towels.

Heat the oil in a large, heavy saucepan over medium-high heat until it reaches 375 degrees F, about 8 minutes. Use a kitchen thermometer to determine when the oil has reached the correct temperature. If you don't have a kitchen thermometer, test the temperature by adding a small piece of sweet potato. If it sizzles vigorously, the oil is hot enough.

Carefully lower the potatoes into the oil and fry until crispy, about 10 minutes. Remove the potatoes with a metal slotted spoon and transfer to the lined plate. Let drain for about 1 minute.

Transfer to the bowl with the spice mixture. Use tongs to gently toss the fries with the spices until evenly coated. If desired, add more pepper to taste and toss again.

BAKED CURRIED SWEET TATER FRIES: Preheat the oven to 425 degrees F and line a baking sheet with parchment paper. Cut the potatoes as directed and combine the curry powder, paprika, cumin, salt, cayenne, and pepper in a small bowl. Put the sweet potatoes in a large bowl, drizzle 1 tablespoon of extra-virgin olive oil over them, and toss until evenly coated. Sprinkle the spice mixture over the potatoes and toss to coat. Transfer the potatoes to the lined baking sheet and bake for 45 to 50 minutes, until crispy, flipping the potatoes halfway through the baking time.

Per serving (based on 3 servings): 496 calories, 3 g protein, 38 g fat (3 g sat), 33 g carbs, 414 mg sodium, 59 mg calcium, 5 g fiber

In case you're unfamiliar with green tomatoes, they're simply unripe tomatoes. If you grow tomatoes, then you have a ready source; otherwise, look for them at farmers' markets. You're especially likely to find them just before the first frost, when there isn't enough time left for them to ripen.

Fried Green Tomatoes

MAKES 4 HELPIN'S

2 large green tomatoes

½ teaspoon salt, plus more
    for sprinkling

½ cup cornstarch

¾ cup unsweetened soy milk

½ cup cornmeal

¼ cup panko breadcrumbs

½ teaspoon garlic powder

½ teaspoon onion powder

½ teaspoon paprika

¼ teaspoon ground pepper

¼ cup canola oil, plus more
    if needed

Cut the tomatoes into thick slices. Sprinkle each slice with salt.

Put the cornstarch in a wide, shallow bowl. Pour the soy milk into another wide, shallow bowl. Put the cornmeal, panko, garlic powder, onion powder, paprika, pepper, and ½ teaspoon of salt in a third shallow bowl and mix well.

Line a plate with several layers of paper towels.

Heat the oil in a large, heavy skillet over medium heat. The oil should generously coat the bottom of the skillet; if it doesn't, add more oil as needed, 1 tablespoon at a time. Sprinkle a pinch of flour over the oil to check the heat. If the oil sizzles, it's ready.

Dip a slice of tomato in the cornstarch, coating both sides, then dip it in the soy milk. Dredge it in the cornmeal mixture, coating both sides evenly. Carefully lower it into the skillet. Repeat until the skillet is full but not overcrowded; the slices shouldn't touch or overlap. You may have to cook the tomatoes in two batches.

Fry the tomatoes until brown on the bottom, 3 to 5 minutes. Flip and fry until the other side is brown, about 3 minutes. Transfer to the lined plate to drain.

Per serving: 306 calories, 4 g protein, 16 g fat (1 g sat), 35 g carbs, 313 mg sodium, 25 mg calcium, 2 g fiber

Everything tastes better deep-fried—especially tender summer squash. Crispy slices of fried squash are the perfect accompaniment to any Southern entrée.

Fried Squash

1 cup unsweetened soy milk

1 teaspoon cider vinegar

2 cups whole wheat pastry flour

1 tablespoon plus 1 teaspoon onion powder

2 teaspoons dried parsley

2 teaspoons ground pepper

½ teaspoon salt, plus more if desired

3 cups canola oil

4 medium summer squash, thinly sliced

Put the soy milk and vinegar in a shallow bowl and stir well. Set aside until the soy milk curdles and thickens, about 2 minutes.

Put the flour, onion powder, parsley, pepper, and salt in a medium bowl and mix well.

Line a plate with several layers of paper towels.

Heat the oil in a large, heavy saucepan over high heat until it reaches 375 degrees F, about 8 minutes. Use a kitchen thermometer to determine when the oil has reached the correct temperature. If you don't have a kitchen thermometer, test the temperature by adding a small piece of squash. If it sizzles vigorously, the oil is hot enough.

Dip a slice of squash in the soy milk mixture and then in the flour mixture, coating both sides evenly. Carefully lower it into the skillet from just above the surface of the oil. Bubbles should immediately form around the squash; if they don't, give the oil a few more minutes to heat. Repeat until the saucepan is as full as possible. You'll probably have to cook the squash in two or three batches.

Fry until golden brown, 7 to 10 minutes. Remove the squash using a metal slotted spoon and transfer to the lined plate to drain. Season with more salt to taste if desired.

Per serving (based on 7 servings): 308 calories, 6 g protein, 17 g fat (1 g sat), 32 g carbs, 179 mg sodium, 57 mg calcium, 6 g fiber

've lived in the South my whole life, but I'd never heard of fried cucumbers until I met my friend Wes, a humble country cook whose tasty meals could rival Paula Deen's any day. When he asked me if I was going to include fried cucumbers in my cookbook, I had to admit that I'd never heard of such a thing. He explained the basic recipe framework, and I veganized the batter and subbed whole wheat pastry flour for the white flour in his recipe. Who says fried foods can't be a little bit healthy? Dip these in Country Buttermilk Ranch Dressing (page 9) for a tasty side dish or appetizer.

Fried Cucumbers

MAKES 4 TO 6 HELPIN'S

1 cup unsweetened soy milk

1 tablespoon cider vinegar

2 cups whole wheat pastry flour

4 teaspoons onion powder

2 teaspoons dried dill weed

2 teaspoons garlic powder

½ teaspoon salt, plus more if desired

½ teaspoon ground pepper

¼ cup canola oil, plus more if needed

4 pickling cucumbers, scrubbed and sliced ¼ inch thick

Put the soy milk and vinegar in a shallow bowl and stir well. Set aside until the soy milk curdles and thickens, about 2 minutes.

Put the flour, onion powder, dill weed, garlic powder, salt, and pepper in a medium bowl and mix well.

Line a plate with several layers of paper towels.

Heat the oil in a large, heavy skillet over medium heat. The oil should generously coat the bottom of the skillet; if it doesn't, add more oil as needed, 1 tablespoon at a time. Sprinkle a pinch of flour over the oil to check the heat. If the oil sizzles, it's ready.

Dip a slice of cucumber in the soy milk mixture and then in the flour mixture, coating both sides evenly. Repeat the process, dipping the same cucumber slice in the soy milk mixture and the flour a second time. Carefully lower it into the skillet. Repeat until the skillet is full but not overcrowded; the slices shouldn't touch or overlap. You may have to fry the cucumbers in batches.

Fry the cucumbers until golden brown and crispy on the bottom, 3 to 4 minutes. Flip and fry until the other side is golden brown and crispy, about 3 minutes. Transfer to the lined plate to drain. Season with more salt to taste if desired.

Per serving (based on 5 servings): 326 calories, 8 g protein, 13 g fat (1 g sat), 44 g carbs, 238 mg sodium, 74 mg calcium, 7 g fiber

Macaroni and tomatoes is a staple dish in my mama's repertoire, and in the South, we often eat it as a side dish. When I was kid, I opted for a bowl instead of a plate to hold my serving of tender macaroni and stewed tomatoes because I didn't want to miss out on the yummy tomato broth. Here I've re-created that treasured family recipe using juicy summer tomatoes and fresh basil. I recommend making this dish only when tomatoes are in season.

Mama's Mac and Tomatoes

Advance preparation required   **MAKES 4 TO 6 HELPIN'S**

8 large tomatoes

1 cup water, plus more if needed

8 ounces quinoa macaroni or whole wheat macaroni

2 tablespoons chopped fresh basil

1 tablespoon extra-virgin olive oil

½ teaspoon salt

Ground pepper

Put the tomatoes in a large pot and add just enough water to cover them. Bring to a boil over high heat, then decrease the heat to medium-high and boil for 1 minute. Drain in a colander and run cold water over the tomatoes until they're cool enough to handle. Peel the tomatoes (the skins should slip off easily) and discard the skins. Cut the tomatoes into quarters.

Return the tomatoes to the pot and add the water. Bring to a boil over high heat. Decrease the heat to medium-low, cover, and simmer until the tomatoes are very soft and broken down, 45 to 60 minutes, checking the water level periodically. If the water has cooked off and the tomatoes are sticking, add more water, about ¼ cup at a time. The tomatoes should be thick and saucy, so only add enough water to prevent sticking.

Bring a large pot of salted water to a boil over high heat. Stir in the macaroni. Decrease the heat to medium-low and cook, stirring occasionally, until tender but firm. Drain well. Add the macaroni, basil, oil, and salt to the tomatoes and stir gently until well combined. Season with pepper to taste.

Per serving (based on 5 servings): 231 calories, 9 g protein, 4 g fat (0 g sat), 42 g carbs, 239 mg sodium, 31 mg calcium, 4 g fiber

Earthy sage and mushrooms combine with toasted pecans and nutrient-packed quinoa for a savory fall or winter side dish. In fact, the hearty flavors reminiscent of stuffing make this an appropriate dish for a vegan Thanksgiving dinner. But don't hesitate to whip up this easy grain dish as an accompaniment for a summer meal instead.

Nutty Mushroom Quinoa

MAKES 5 TO 6 HELPIN'S

2 cups low-sodium vegetable broth

1 cup quinoa

½ cup chopped pecans

2 tablespoons nonhydrogenated vegan margarine

1 small yellow onion, chopped

2 cloves garlic, minced

3 cups sliced button mushrooms

1 teaspoon rubbed sage

¼ teaspoon salt

¼ teaspoon dried tarragon

2 tablespoons white cooking wine

Ground pepper

Pour the broth into a medium saucepan and bring to a boil over high heat. Stir in the quinoa and decrease the heat to low. Cover and cook until the quinoa is tender and the liquid is absorbed, about 20 minutes.

Toast the pecans in a dry skillet over low heat, stirring frequently, until lightly browned and fragrant, about 5 minutes.

Melt the margarine in a large skillet over medium heat. Add the onion and cook, stirring frequently, for 2 to 3 minutes. Add the garlic and cook, stirring frequently, for 1 minute. Add the mushrooms and cook, stirring frequently, until they begin to cook down, about 5 minutes.

Stir in the sage, salt, and tarragon. Cook, stirring frequently, for 3 minutes. Add the wine and cook, stirring frequently, for 3 minutes. Remove from the heat.

Add the quinoa and pecans and mix well. Season with pepper to taste.

Per serving (based on 5.5 servings): 241 calories, 7 g protein, 13 g fat (2 g sat), 21 g carbs, 228 mg sodium, 34 mg calcium, 4 g fiber

For this spicy side dish, I fused the flavor of Cajun dirty rice with the tomato-based Spanish rice often found in Mexican restaurants. I call it Dirty South fusion cuisine.

Dirty (South) Rice

MAKES 4 TO 6 HELPIN'S

2¼ cups low-sodium vegetable broth

1 cup brown rice

1 small yellow onion, chopped

1 can (4 ounces) **diced green chiles,** drained

2 tablespoons no-salt-added tomato paste

1 tablespoon nonhydrogenated vegan margarine

2 cloves garlic, minced

1 teaspoon chili powder

½ teaspoon Cajun seasoning, plus more if desired

½ teaspoon dried basil

2 Roma tomatoes, diced

½ cup frozen corn kernels, thawed

Salt

Ground pepper

Hot sauce

Put the broth, rice, onion, chiles, tomato paste, margarine, garlic, chili powder, Cajun seasoning, and basil in a large saucepan and mix well. Bring to a boil over high heat. Decrease the heat to medium-low, cover, and cook until the rice is tender and the liquid is absorbed, 45 to 50 minutes. Remove from the heat.

Stir in the tomatoes and corn. Season with salt, pepper, and more Cajun seasoning to taste. Serve with hot sauce.

Per serving (based on 5 servings): 202 calories, 6 g protein, 4 g fat (1 g sat), 37 g carbs, 235 mg sodium, 27 mg calcium, 4 g fiber

DAILY BREAD

BISCUITS, LOAVES, AND CORNBREAD

Every Southern cook should know how to make at least two breads from scratch: fluffy buttermilk biscuits and crumbly cornbread. This brief bread chapter only contains the basics. I'm no baker, so I tend to buy French bread and sandwich loaves from a store. But my biscuits and cornbread are always homemade.

Try the Whole Wheat Buttermilk Biscuits (page 136) or the Jalapeño-Corn Buttermilk Cornbread (page 137) for a more healthful twist on white-flour breads. Fry up a batch of Hoecakes (page 138) as an alternative to cornbread, or bake some Hush Puppy Corn Muffins (page 139) in lieu of typical deep-fried hush puppies.

You'll be glad to know that none of these recipes involve much fuss. Now you can whip up your own daily bread to accompany all of your home-cooked Southern meals.

very good Southern belle has her own secret recipe for buttermilk biscuits. But I'm sharin' mine with y'all, so I guess it isn't a secret anymore. Smother these with Sausage Gravy with Sage (page 24) or Chocolate Gravy (page 23), stuff 'em with vegan sausage and grape jelly, or try my Southern Tofu Chicken Biscuits (page 34).

Whole Wheat Buttermilk Biscuits

See photo facing page 22.

MAKES 8 LARGE OR 16 SMALL BISCUITS

1 cup unsweetened soy milk

2 teaspoons cider vinegar

2½ cups whole wheat pastry flour, plus more for dusting

1 tablespoon baking powder

¾ teaspoon salt

½ teaspoon baking soda

3 tablespoons nonhydrogenated vegetable shortening

2 tablespoons nonhydrogenated vegan margarine

Preheat the oven to 425 degrees F.

Put the soy milk and vinegar in a small bowl and stir well. Set aside until the soy milk curdles and thickens, about 2 minutes.

Sift the flour, baking powder, salt, and baking soda into a large bowl and mix well. Add the shortening and margarine and cut them in with a pastry blender or your hands until the texture resembles coarse crumbs.

Pour in the soy milk mixture and mix well. You'll need to dig in with your hands and lightly knead the mixture in the bowl to make sure all the ingredients are well combined. Don't overmix, or the biscuits won't be light and fluffy. Sprinkle a couple of generous pinches of flour over the top of the dough while it's still in the bowl, but don't mix it in.

Transfer the dough to a liberally floured work surface (a generous amount of flour is needed because the dough tends to be a little sticky). Lightly roll out or pat down the dough until it's about ¾ inch thick.

Cut out biscuits with a 2- or 3-inch biscuit cutter or round cookie cutter, depending on the desired size of biscuits. Press the cutter into the dough and then lift it straight up. Don't twist the cutter, or the baked biscuits will be flat. Carefully transfer the cut biscuits to a baking sheet. Gather up the remaining bits of dough. Roll out or pat down until ¾ inch thick and cut the last few biscuits.

Bake for 12 to 15 minutes, until golden brown.

Per (large) biscuit: 254 calories, 6 g protein, 14 g fat (4 g sat), 25 g carbs, 460 mg sodium, 150 mg calcium, 5 g fiber

This cornbread is baked in a cast-iron skillet for a crispy crust and a melt-in-your-mouth, tender interior. Try crumblin' a slice into a bowl of soup beans, such as Chipotle Chickpea Chili (page 76) or Harvest Crowder Peas (page 72).

Jalapeño-Corn Buttermilk Cornbread

MAKES 8 HELPIN'S

1 cup unsweetened soy milk

1 tablespoon cider vinegar

1 cup yellow cornmeal

1 cup whole wheat pastry flour

2 tablespoons sugar

2 teaspoons baking powder

1 teaspoon baking soda

½ teaspoon salt

¼ cup warm water

1 tablespoon Ener-G egg replacer

1 tablespoon canola oil

1 cup frozen corn kernels, thawed

¼ cup chopped pickled jalapeño chiles

Preheat the oven to 400 degrees F. Generously coat a 10-inch cast-iron skillet with nonhydrogenated vegan margarine or spray it with cooking spray.

Put the soy milk and vinegar in a small bowl and stir well. Set aside until the soy milk curdles and thickens, about 2 minutes.

Put the cornmeal, flour, sugar, baking powder, baking soda, and salt in a large bowl and mix well.

Put the water and egg replacer in a medium bowl and whisk until the egg replacer is dissolved and the mixture is foamy. Stir in the soy milk mixture and oil. Pour into the cornmeal mixture and stir until just combined. Don't overmix. Add the corn and chiles and stir until just combined.

Pour the batter into the prepared skillet and spread it in an even layer. Bake for 30 minutes, until a toothpick inserted in the center comes out clean. Slice into 8 wedges.

Per serving: 171 calories, 5 g protein, 3 g fat (0 g sat), 30 g carbs, 473 mg sodium, 107 mg calcium, 4 g fiber

ankees call these johnnycakes, but down here in the South, these flat cornbread pancakes are known as hoecakes. Whatever you call 'em, they're quick to make and delicious as an accompaniment to a bowl of hot beans or vegetable soup.

Hoecakes

MAKES 8 TO 10 HOECAKES

1 cup yellow cornmeal

¼ cup whole wheat pastry flour

1 tablespoon sugar

1 teaspoon baking powder

½ teaspoon salt

¼ cup water

2 tablespoons ground flaxseeds

1 cup unsweetened soy milk

¼ cup canola oil, plus more if needed

Put the cornmeal, flour, sugar, baking powder, and salt in a large bowl and mix well.

Put the water and flaxseeds in a medium bowl and whisk until well combined. Add the soy milk and whisk again. Pour into the cornmeal mixture and stir until just combined.

Line a plate with several layers of paper towels.

Heat the oil in a large, heavy skillet over medium heat. The oil should generously coat the bottom of the skillet. If it doesn't, add more oil as needed, 1 tablespoon at a time. Sprinkle a pinch of flour over the oil to check the heat. If the oil sizzles, it's ready.

Drop a large spoonful (about 2 tablespoons) of the batter into the skillet by tilting the spoon down so the batter drains from the tip. Repeat until the skillet is full but not overcrowded; the hoecakes shouldn't touch. You may have to cook them in two batches.

Fry until bubbles begin to form on top and the bottoms are lightly browned and crispy, 3 to 4 minutes. Carefully flip and fry until the other side is lightly browned, about 3 minutes. Transfer the hoecakes to the lined plate to drain.

Per hoecake (based on 9 hoecakes): 144 calories, 3 g protein, 9 g fat (1 g sat), 15 g carbs, 176 mg sodium, 50 mg calcium, 2 g fiber

ush puppies are small fried balls of cornmeal batter flecked with minced onion and corn. These muffins have the same ingredients as the traditional fried version, but they're baked so you can enjoy them guilt-free. Serve them with Baked Tofu Fish Fry (page 88) for a classic Southern meal.

Hush Puppy Corn Muffins

MAKES 12 MUFFINS

1½ cups yellow cornmeal

½ cup whole wheat pastry flour

1 teaspoon salt

1 teaspoon baking powder

½ teaspoon baking soda

¼ cup warm water

1 tablespoon Ener-G egg replacer

1 can (about 15 ounces) **creamed corn**

½ cup minced onion

2 tablespoons canola oil

1 tablespoon sugar

Preheat the oven to 350 degrees F. Spray a 12-cup standard muffin tin with cooking spray.

Put the cornmeal, flour, salt, baking powder, and baking soda in a large bowl and mix well.

Put the water and egg replacer in a medium bowl and whisk until the egg replacer is dissolved and the mixture is foamy. Stir in the creamed corn, onion, oil, and sugar. Pour into the cornmeal mixture and stir until just combined. Don't overmix.

Spoon the batter into the muffin tin, dividing it evenly among the muffin cups and filling each cup about three-quarters full. Bake for 25 minutes, until a toothpick inserted in the center of a muffin comes out clean.

Per muffin: 163 calories, 3 g protein, 3 g fat (0 g sat), 29 g carbs, 270 mg sodium, 41 mg calcium, 4 g fiber

aking homemade yeast bread takes a ton of patience with all that rising and kneading business. Take a shortcut with this no-knead, no-rise beer bread. I encourage you to experiment with different styles of beer to change up the flavor.

Whole Wheat Beer Bread

MAKES ONE 9-INCH LOAF; 8 TO 10 HELPIN'S

3 cups whole wheat pastry flour

1 tablespoon baking powder

1 tablespoon sugar

½ teaspoon salt

1 (12-ounce) **vegan beer** (see note), at room temperature

1 tablespoon nonhydrogenated vegan margarine, melted

Preheat the oven to 350 degrees F. Spray a 9 x 5-inch loaf pan with cooking spray.

Put the flour, baking powder, sugar, and salt in a large bowl and mix well. Slowly pour in the beer, taking care to not let it foam. If it does get foamy, wait a few seconds for the bubbles to die down. Stir until a ball of dough forms.

Transfer the dough to the prepared pan and spread it evenly. Bake for 30 minutes. Brush the top of the bread with the margarine and bake for 25 minutes longer, until the top is golden brown and a toothpick inserted in the center comes out clean.

NOTE: Any type or flavor of beer works well for this recipe. Darker brews will lend a more complex, nutty flavor to the bread, whereas lighter beers will result in bread with a milder, hoppy flavor. For a comprehensive list of vegan beers, go to barnivore.com.

Per serving (based on 9 servings): 181 calories, 4 g protein, 2 g fat (0 g sat), 34 g carbs, 254 mg sodium, 141 mg calcium, 5 g fiber

affles aren't just for dousing with syrup anymore. They also make great sandwich bread, even for savory fillings. Try these for Fried Tofu Chicken Wafflewiches with Maple-Mustard Sauce (page 64), or stuff 'em with anything you like: peanut butter, vegan deli slices, or vegan burgers. You can even use 'em to make a vegan grilled cheese sandwich.

Savory Sandwich Waffles

MAKES 4 WAFFLES; ENOUGH FOR 2 SANDWICHES

1 cup unsweetened soy milk

1½ teaspoons cider vinegar

2 tablespoons water

1 tablespoon ground flaxseeds

1 cup whole wheat pastry flour

½ teaspoon baking powder

¼ teaspoon salt

2 tablespoons canola oil

Spray a waffle iron with cooking spray and heat according to the manufacturer's instructions.

Put the soy milk and vinegar in a small bowl and stir well. Set aside until the soy milk curdles and thickens, about 2 minutes.

Combine the water and flaxseeds in a small bowl and mix well.

Put the flour, baking powder, and salt in a large bowl and mix well.

Pour the oil and the flaxseed mixture into the soy milk mixture and stir until thoroughly blended. Pour into the flour mixture and stir until just combined. Don't overmix.

Pour one-quarter of the batter into the waffle iron and cook according to the manufacturer's instructions. Repeat with the remaining batter, spraying the waffle iron with more cooking spray after removing each waffle.

Per waffle: 214 calories, 6 g protein, 9 g fat (1 g sat), 27 g carbs, 205 mg sodium, 83 mg calcium, 5 g fiber

SWEET ENDINGS

DECADENT DESSERTS

Without my beloved granny, this dessert chapter probably wouldn't have happened. A kitchen pioneer of extraordinary talents, my granny spent endless hours piddlin' away in her kitchen to veganize her delicious pies and cakes.

The Coconut Icebox Cake (page 157) and Fresh Strawberry Pie (page 147) are among my favorites of Granny's veganized desserts, but her Mandarin Orange Cobbler (page 145) and Chocolate Fudgy Puddin' Cake (page 153) are equally delicious.

A few of my inventions—the Peanut Butter and Banana Cupcakes with Peanut Buttercream (page 158), Mint Julep Brownies (page 164), and Holy Mole Chocolate-Chile Cupcakes with Cinnamon Buttercream (page 160)—are pretty darn tasty as well. So save room for dessert!

y mom has been using this basic cobbler recipe for years, long before she knew what "vegan" meant. I guess you could say it's accidentally vegan. The only change I've made is substituting whole wheat pastry flour for the all-purpose flour in her recipe. You can use this basic recipe to make any kind of fresh fruit cobbler, but the deep-purple blackberry juice peeking through the flaky crust is a sight to behold—and a sweet pleasure to taste!

Whole Wheat Blackberry Cobbler

MAKES 6 TO 8 HELPIN'S

4 cups fresh blackberries

¾ to 1 cup sugar, plus 1 tablespoon for sprinkling

1 tablespoon freshly squeezed lemon juice

2 tablespoons nonhydrogenated vegan margarine

1 cup whole wheat pastry flour, plus more for sprinkling

¼ teaspoon salt

⅓ cup nonhydrogenated vegetable shortening

2 tablespoons cold water

Preheat the oven to 350 degrees F. Spray a 2½-quart casserole dish with cooking spray.

Put the blackberries, ¾ cup of the sugar, and the lemon juice in a large bowl and stir gently until thoroughly combined. Taste and add up to ¼ cup more sugar if desired; the amount of sugar needed depends on the tartness of the berries. Transfer the berries and their juices to the prepared casserole dish. Top with the margarine, putting dabs of it evenly over the berries.

Put the flour and salt in a medium bowl and mix well. Add the shortening and cut it in with a pastry blender or your hands until the texture resembles coarse crumbs. Sprinkle the water over the mixture and stir until a dough forms. Shape the dough into a ball.

Sprinkle a little flour on a sheet of waxed paper (see note) or a clean work surface and put the dough on the floured surface. Sprinkle a few pinches of flour over the dough, then flatten the dough with your hands. Use a rolling pin to roll the dough out to just fit inside the casserole dish over the berries without draping over the sides; it's okay if the crust doesn't quite reach the edges of the pan.

Lay the crust over the berries. Sprinkle a few drops of water over the crust, then sprinkle the remaining tablespoon of sugar evenly over the top. Bake for 45 minutes, until the crust is golden brown and the juices are bubbling.

NOTE: If you use waxed paper to roll out the dough, sprinkle a little water on the countertop first to keep the waxed paper from sliding.

Per serving (based on 7 servings): 305 calories, 3 g protein, 13 g fat (5 g sat), 43 g carbs, 111 mg sodium, 36 mg calcium, 7 g fiber

y granny invented this cakey orange cobbler as a twist on peach cobbler. Be sure to purchase canned mandarin oranges that are packed in their own juice rather than sugar syrup.

Mandarin Orange Cobbler

MAKES 4 HELPIN'S

2 tablespoons nonhydrogenated vegan margarine, melted

¾ cup whole wheat pastry flour

½ cup plus 1 tablespoon sugar

1 teaspoon baking powder

¼ teaspoon salt

¾ cup plain soy milk

1 can (about 10 ounces) **mandarin oranges, drained**

Preheat the oven to 350 degrees F.

Put the margarine in a 1½-quart casserole dish and turn the pan from side to side to coat the bottom and sides with the margarine.

Put the flour, ½ cup of the sugar, and the baking powder and salt in a medium bowl and mix well. Add the soy milk and stir until just combined.

Pour the batter into the prepared casserole dish. Top with the mandarin oranges, spacing them evenly over the surface. They will begin to sink into the batter, and that's okay. Sprinkle the remaining tablespoon of sugar evenly over the top.

Bake for 50 minutes, until the top is golden brown and the center is set and springs back when touched lightly.

Per serving: 196 calories, 4 g protein, 7 g fat (2 g sat), 58 g carbs, 309 mg sodium, 138 mg calcium, 4 g fiber

his simple crust is made with whole wheat pastry flour rather than all-purpose flour. Even though pie isn't exactly health food, subbing whole wheat pastry flour helps a little. Be sure to use whole wheat pastry flour and not regular whole wheat flour, as it has a lower protein content, making it preferable for tender baked treats. Recipes in this book specify whether to use a single or double crust. If you need a double crust, just double the amounts of all the ingredients, then divide the dough into two equal portions and roll them out as directed.

Whole Wheat Pie Crust

MAKES 1 PIE CRUST

1 cup whole wheat pastry flour, plus more for sprinkling

¼ teaspoon salt

⅓ cup nonhydrogenated vegetable shortening

2 tablespoons cold water

Put the flour and salt in a medium bowl. Add the shortening and cut it in with a pastry blender or your hands until the texture resembles coarse crumbs. Sprinkle the water over the mixture and stir until a dough forms. Shape the dough into a ball.

Sprinkle a little flour on a sheet of waxed paper (see notes) or a clean work surface and put the dough on the floured surface. Sprinkle a few pinches of flour over the dough, then flatten the dough with your hands. Use a rolling pin to roll it out to a 9- or 10-inch circle, depending on the size of pie pan specified in the recipe. Rolling a circle takes practice, so don't fret if the result isn't perfectly round.

To line a pie pan, put the rolled dough over the bottom and up the side of the pan and crimp the edge with a fork.

NOTES

- If you use waxed paper to roll out the dough, sprinkle a little water on the countertop first to keep the waxed paper from sliding.

- For a double-crust pie, line the pan with the first crust and don't crimp the edge. Roll out the second crust and lay it over the filled pie. Trim away any dough that hangs over the edge of the pan, then seal the edge by crimping the two layers of dough together with a fork.

- If you're making a pie with a no-bake filling, you'll need to bake the crust first. Preheat the oven to 375 degrees F. Use a fork to poke a few tiny holes in the bottom of the crust. Bake for 15 to 17 minutes, until golden brown, or as directed in the pie recipe. Let cool before filling.

Per serving (based on 7 servings): 141 calories, 2 g protein, 10 g fat (4 g sat), 13 g carbs, 76 mg sodium, 11 mg calcium, 2 g fiber

ack in the day, my granny used strawberry gelatin in this family recipe, but now she substitutes cornstarch to make it vegan. Since this pie allows the sweet flavor of fresh strawberries to shine, I recommend making it only when strawberries are in season.

Fresh Strawberry Pie

MAKES ONE 9-INCH PIE; 6 TO 8 HELPIN'S

1 store-bought vegan pie crust or
Whole Wheat Pie Crust (page 146)

1 cup water

1 cup sugar

¼ cup cornstarch

4 cups strawberries, hulled and
thinly sliced

Preheat the oven to 375 degrees F. Use a fork to poke a few tiny holes in the bottom of the pie crust.

Bake the pie crust for 15 to 17 minutes, until golden brown. Let cool completely.

Put the water in a medium saucepan and bring to a boil over medium-high heat. Decrease the heat to medium.

Put the sugar and cornstarch in a small bowl and mix well. Add to the boiling water in a slow, steady stream, whisking all the while. Cook, whisking constantly, until the mixture forms a very thick gel and drips off a spoon in globs, 5 to 10 minutes.

Remove from the heat and stir in the strawberries. Pour into the pie crust and refrigerate until the filling is firm, 1 to 2 hours (see note).

NOTE: If the filling doesn't firm up, the cornstarch mixture may not have been cooked long enough. But never fear—you have a second chance. Remove the strawberries with a slotted spoon and pour the filling mixture back into a saucepan. Cook over medium heat, whisking constantly, until thick. Stir the strawberries back into the mixture, then pour it back into the crust. Refrigerate for 1 to 2 hours, until firm.

Per serving (based on 7 servings): 295 calories, 2 g protein, 10 g fat (4 g sat), 50 g carbs, 79 mg sodium, 26 mg calcium, 4 g fiber

**M**y granny used to manage a department store, and the ladies on staff held a pie recipe contest one day. Granny entered her famous marshmallow crème pie with pineapple, and the judges decided it was the hands-down winner. But since Granny worked in management, she didn't feel right about accepting the honor. She wanted a member of her sales staff to win, so she forfeited her prize. Years later, Granny veganized this pie for me, swapping vanilla pudding for the marshmallows. Take one bite and you'll see why this luscious pie is a winner.

Pineapple Cream Pie with Toasted Coconut

MAKES ONE 9-INCH PIE; 6 TO 8 HELPIN'S

½ cup sweetened shredded dried coconut

1 can (8 ounces) **crushed pineapple with juice**

1 package (3.4 ounces) **vanilla instant pudding mix** (see notes)

1 container (10.14 ounces) **vegan whippable topping** (see notes)

1 store-bought vegan graham cracker crust

Toast the coconut in a dry skillet over medium heat, stirring occasionally, until lightly browned and fragrant, about 5 minutes.

Put the crushed pineapple and its juice and the dry instant pudding mix in a medium bowl. (Don't follow the instructions on the box to make pudding.) Mix well.

Put the whippable topping in a large bowl or the bowl of a stand mixer fitted with the whisk attachment. Beat with a handheld mixer or the stand mixer until fluffy. This may take 7 to 10 minutes.

Measure out 2 cups of the whipped topping (reserve any leftover whipped topping for another use) and gently fold it into the pineapple mixture. Transfer the mixture to the crust and spread it in an even layer. Scatter the toasted coconut evenly over the top. Refrigerate until chilled, about 2 hours.

NOTES

- You might be surprised to learn that Jell-O brand instant pudding is vegan.
- Vegan whipped cream comes in prepared form in an upright squirtable canister and in whippable liquid form in a box. For this recipe, you'll need the unprepared, whippable kind, such as Soyatoo or Rich Whip brand.

Per serving (based on 7 servings): 348 calories, 2 g protein, 16 g fat (11 g sat), 47 g carbs, 374 mg sodium, 2 mg calcium, 1 g fiber

y granny weaseled the nonvegan version of this recipe out of a waitress at a steakhouse. Then she ever so lovingly veganized it for a holiday meal so I could join my family for dessert. It quickly became my favorite pie, and my dad's. In the spirit of that nice waitress who shared the original recipe with my granny, I'm sharing it with all of y'all.

Old-Fashioned Coconut Pie

1 cup sugar

¼ cup whole wheat pastry flour

½ teaspoon salt

¾ cup plain soy milk

3 tablespoons Ener-G egg replacer

6 tablespoons nonhydrogenated vegan margarine, at room temperature

1½ cups sweetened shredded dried coconut

1 store-bought vegan pie crust or Whole Wheat Pie Crust, unbaked (page 146)

Preheat the oven to 325 degrees F.

Combine the sugar, flour, and salt in a small bowl.

Put ¼ cup of the soy milk and the egg replacer in a large bowl or the bowl of a stand mixer and whisk until the egg replacer is dissolved and the mixture is foamy. Add the margarine and beat with a handheld mixer or the stand mixer until creamy. Add the remaining ½ cup of soy milk and beat until thoroughly blended. Add the flour mixture and mix until just combined. Stir in 1 cup of the coconut.

Transfer the mixture to the pie crust and spread it in an even layer. Scatter the remaining ½ cup of coconut evenly over the top. Bake for 1 hour, until the coconut is golden brown and the filling is firm (it will firm up further as it cools). Let cool before serving.

Per serving (based on 7 servings): 451 calories, 4 g protein, 24 g fat (12 g sat), 56 g carbs, 394 mg sodium, 25 mg calcium, 4 g fiber

fter tasting this pie, a friend exclaimed, "I would eat this pie every day if I could!" This veganized version of my granny's pineapple pie is perfect for hotter-than-hot Southern nights when the humidity makes you feel like you're in the tropics.

Pineapple Custard Pie

MAKES ONE 9-INCH PIE; 6 TO 8 HELPIN'S

¾ cup plain soy milk

3 tablespoons Ener-G egg replacer

1 cup sugar

½ cup whole wheat pastry flour

6 tablespoons nonhydrogenated vegan margarine, at room temperature

1 can (20 ounces) crushed pineapple

1 store-bought vegan pie crust or Whole Wheat Pie Crust (page 146), unbaked

4 pineapple rings

5 maraschino cherries

Preheat the oven to 350 degrees F.

Put ½ cup of the soy milk and the egg replacer in a large bowl or the bowl of a stand mixer fitted with the paddle attachment and whisk until the egg replacer is dissolved and the mixture is foamy. Add the sugar and flour and beat with a handheld mixer or the stand mixer until thoroughly blended. Add the margarine and the remaining ¼ cup of soy milk and beat until creamy.

Drain the pineapple in a colander, then use your hands to squeeze out as much juice as possible. Stir the pineapple into the sugar mixture.

Pour the mixture into the pie crust and spread it in an even layer. Bake for 20 minutes. Remove the pie from the oven and put the pineapple rings on top, placing them side-by-side to form a square.

Return the pie to the oven and bake for 40 minutes, until the filling is somewhat firm and the crust is golden brown. Remove the pie from the oven. Place a cherry in the center of each pineapple ring and place the remaining cherry in the center of the pie. Let cool before serving.

Per serving (based on 7 servings): 462 calories, 4 g protein, 20 g fat (7 g sat), 69 g carbs, 207 mg sodium, 27 mg calcium, 4 g fiber

Smoky Stewed Okra and Tomatoes, *page 125,*
and Cheesy Twice-Baked Taters with Leeks and Dill, *page 126.*

"Elvis Cupcakes"
(Peanut Butter and Banana Cupcakes with Peanut Buttercream, *page 158*)

This ain't your grandma's pecan pie. With dark chocolate chunks, toasted pecans, and dark rum, this pie is a force to be reckoned with. You'll want to stay on its good side. For an extra-special treat, serve it with vegan ice cream.

Tipsy Dark Chocolate Pecan Pie

MAKES ONE 9-INCH PIE; 6 TO 8 HELPIN'S

1 store-bought vegan pie crust or Whole Wheat Pie Crust, unbaked (page 146)

2 cups pecan halves

¾ cup plus 3 tablespoons plain soy milk

½ cup cornstarch

½ cup dark chocolate chips or chunks, at least 60 percent cacao

½ cup maple syrup

¼ cup blackstrap molasses

2 tablespoons nonhydrogenated vegan margarine

1 teaspoon vanilla extract

1 tablespoon dark rum

Preheat the oven to 350 degrees F. Use a fork to poke a few tiny holes in the bottom of the pie crust.

Bake the pie crust for 10 minutes. Let cool.

Spread 1 cup of the pecans on a baking sheet and toast them in the oven for 10 minutes. This step can be done while the pie crust is baking. Leave the oven on.

Put ¾ cup of the soy milk and the cornstarch in a small bowl and stir until the cornstarch is dissolved.

Put the remaining 3 tablespoons of soy milk and the chocolate in a medium saucepan over low heat. Stir constantly until the chocolate is melted. Stir in the maple syrup and molasses and increase the heat to medium. Add the cornstarch mixture and cook, stirring constantly with a whisk, until very thick, 7 to 10 minutes. Remove from the heat. Add the margarine, vanilla extract, and rum and mix well. Stir in the toasted pecans.

Transfer the mixture to the pie crust and spread it in an even layer. Decorate the top with the remaining cup of pecans by placing them around the outer edge of the filling to form a circle. Make a smaller circle of pecans inside that circle, and continue making concentric circles of pecans until you reach the center.

Bake for 30 minutes, until the pecans are toasted and the filling is firm (it will firm up further as it cools). Let cool for at least 1 hour before serving.

Per serving (based on 7 servings): 607 calories, 7 g protein, 40 g fat (10 g sat), 55 g carbs, 135 mg sodium, 163 mg calcium, 6 g fiber

**B**read puddin' is a yummy (and cost-effective) way to put dessert on the table while also using up stale bread. Many bread puddin's feature cinnamon or rum-raisin flavors, but this version is more reminiscent of a homemade chocolate chip cookie. Topping it with the vanilla sauce takes this humble dessert to a gourmet level.

Chocolate Chip Coconut Bread Puddin'

MAKES 6 HELPIN'S

BREAD PUDDIN'

6 cups cubed stale French bread or sourdough bread

½ cup semisweet chocolate chips

½ cup unsweetened shredded dried coconut

2½ cups plain soy milk, at room temperature

½ cup maple syrup

2 tablespoons nonhydrogenated vegan margarine, melted

1 teaspoon vanilla extract

VANILLA SAUCE

1 cup confectioners' sugar

2 tablespoons plain soy milk

1 teaspoon vanilla extract

To make the bread puddin', preheat the oven to 350 degrees F. Spray a 2½-quart casserole dish with cooking spray.

Put the bread cubes in the prepared casserole dish and sprinkle the chocolate chips and coconut evenly over the top.

Put the soy milk, maple syrup, margarine, and vanilla extract in a medium bowl and mix well. Pour the mixture evenly over the bread cubes, making sure all of the bread gets wet. Bake uncovered for 40 minutes, until the top is golden brown and most of the liquid has been absorbed by the bread.

To make the vanilla sauce, put the confectioners' sugar, soy milk, and vanilla extract in a medium bowl and stir until the sugar dissolves.

To serve, top each helping of warm bread puddin' with 1 to 2 tablespoons of the sauce just before serving.

Per serving: 512 calories, 9 g protein, 22 g fat (15 g sat), 67 g carbs, 258 mg sodium, 74 mg calcium, 4 g fiber

an't choose between cake and pudding? Why not have both? A moist layer of chocolate cake tops a creamy layer of rich, fudgy pudding in this decadent dessert. Top with a scoop of vegan vanilla ice cream for triple dessert action.

Chocolate Fudgy Puddin' Cake

MAKES 1 CAKE; 8 TO 10 HELPIN'S

1 cup whole wheat pastry flour

1¼ cups sugar

7 tablespoons unsweetened cocoa powder

2 teaspoons baking powder

2 teaspoons instant coffee granules

¼ teaspoon salt

½ cup plain soy milk

⅓ cup nonhydrogenated vegan margarine, at room temperature

1½ teaspoons vanilla extract

⅓ cup brown sugar

1¼ cups hot water

Preheat the oven to 350 degrees F. Spray an 8-inch square baking pan with cooking spray.

Put the flour, ¾ cup of the sugar, 3 tablespoons of the cocoa powder, the baking powder, 1 teaspoon of the instant coffee, and the salt in a medium bowl and mix well.

Put the soy milk, margarine, and vanilla extract in a large bowl or the bowl of a stand mixer fitted with the paddle attachment. Beat with a handheld mixer or the stand mixer until thoroughly blended. Add the flour mixture and mix until just combined. Pour the batter into the prepared pan and spread it in an even layer.

Put the remaining ½ cup of sugar, the brown sugar, the remaining 4 tablespoons of cocoa powder, and the remaining teaspoon of instant coffee in a small bowl and mix well. Sprinkle the mixture evenly over the batter. Pour the hot water evenly over the top. Don't stir. As the cake bakes, the ingredients on top will sink to form a pudding layer and the cake will rise to the top.

Bake for about 40 minutes, until the center is almost set. Let stand for 15 minutes. Serve warm.

Per serving (based on 9 servings): 258 calories, 3 g protein, 7 g fat (2 g sat), 47 g carbs, 216 mg sodium, 101 mg calcium, 3 g fiber

Sorghum syrup, a popular natural sweetener in the South, is similar to molasses in taste and consistency. Typically, this type of moist sorghum cake is served sans frosting, which gives you the chance to top it with vegan margarine or vegan cream cheese. Or try it my way: with a dollop of vegan whipped cream and fresh berries. It's also delicious on its own, without any topping.

Sweet Sorghum Cake

MAKES 1 CAKE; 6 TO 8 HELPIN'S

½ cup plain soy milk

1½ teaspoons cider vinegar

2 tablespoons water

1 tablespoon ground flaxseeds

⅓ cup nonhydrogenated vegetable shortening

½ cup sugar

½ cup sorghum syrup or blackstrap molasses

1 cup unbleached all-purpose flour

¾ cup whole wheat pastry flour

1 teaspoon baking soda

1 teaspoon ground cinnamon

1 teaspoon ground ginger

½ teaspoon salt

Preheat the oven to 350 degrees F. Spray an 8-inch square baking pan with cooking spray.

Put the soy milk and vinegar in a small bowl and stir well. Set aside until the soy milk to curdles and thickens, about 2 minutes.

Combine the water and flaxseeds in a small bowl and mix well.

Put the shortening and sugar in a large bowl or the bowl of a stand mixer fitted with the paddle attachment. Beat with a handheld mixer or the stand mixer until creamy. Add the soy milk mixture, flaxseed mixture, and sorghum syrup and beat until combined.

Sift the all-purpose flour, pastry flour, baking soda, cinnamon, ginger, and salt into a medium bowl and mix well. Add to the shortening mixture and mix until just combined. Don't overmix.

Spread the batter in the prepared pan. Bake for 25 to 30 minutes, until a toothpick inserted in the center of the cake comes out clean. Let cool before serving.

Per serving (based on 7 servings): 298 calories, 5 g protein, 11 g fat (4 g sat), 46 g carbs, 341 mg sodium, 18 mg calcium, 3 g fiber

his is a down-home version of banana bread. Although the recipe calls for a ripe banana, the mashed sweet potatoes lend even more moisture, making for a soft, sweet, orange-hued loaf. Spread slices with vegan cream cheese or eat them plain.

Sweet Potato Bread

MAKES 1 LOAF; 8 TO 10 HELPIN'S

2 medium sweet potatoes, peeled and cubed

1 cup chopped pecans

1 very ripe banana

¼ cup canola oil

¼ cup plain soy milk

2 cups whole wheat pastry flour

¾ cup sugar

2 teaspoons baking powder

1 teaspoon ground cinnamon

¾ teaspoon baking soda

½ teaspoon ground ginger

¼ teaspoon salt

Preheat the oven to 350 degrees F. Spray a 9 x 5-inch loaf pan with cooking spray.

Put the sweet potatoes in a large pot and add water to cover. Bring to a boil over high heat. Decrease the heat to medium-low, cover, and cook until fork-tender, about 20 minutes. Drain in a colander.

Spread the pecans on a baking sheet and toast them in the oven for 8 minutes.

Put the potatoes back in the pot and mash with a potato masher or a fork. Measure out 1½ cups of mashed sweet potatoes and put them in a medium bowl (reserve any leftovers for use in another meal). Add the banana and mash again. Stir in the oil and soy milk.

Put the flour, sugar, baking powder, cinnamon, baking soda, ginger, and salt in a large bowl and mix well. Add the sweet potato mixture and stir until just combined. Stir in the pecans.

Spread the batter in the prepared pan. Bake for 60 to 70 minutes, until a toothpick inserted in the center of the loaf comes out clean. Let cool before serving.

Per serving (based on 9 servings): 377 calories, 5 g protein, 16 g fat (1 g sat), 53 g carbs, 265 mg sodium, 123 mg calcium, 7 g fiber

**N**o cookbook would be complete without a recipe for the classic birthday cake—a moist yellow layer cake with creamy chocolate frosting. Down here, we call it yella' cake, but you can say "yellow" if you're not into lazy Southern slang. Top this beauty with rainbow sprinkles for the ultimate birthday (or everyday) treat.

Yella' Cake with Fudgy Frosting

MAKES ONE 2-LAYER CAKE; ABOUT 16 HELPIN'S

CAKE

3 cups unbleached all-purpose flour

2 teaspoons baking powder

½ teaspoon salt

½ teaspoon ground turmeric
(see note)

1½ cups sugar

¾ cup nonhydrogenated vegan margarine

1 cup plain soy milk

½ cup plain nondairy yogurt

1½ teaspoons vanilla extract

FROSTING

2¾ cups confectioners' sugar

⅓ cup plus 1 tablespoon unsweetened cocoa powder

⅓ cup plus 1 tablespoon nonhydrogenated vegan margarine

5 tablespoons plain soy milk

1 teaspoon vanilla extract

To make the cake, preheat the oven to 350 degrees F. Spray two 9-inch round baking pans with cooking spray.

Put the flour, baking powder, salt, and turmeric in a medium bowl and mix well.

Put the sugar and margarine in a large bowl or the bowl of a stand mixer fitted with the paddle attachment. Beat with a handheld mixer or the stand mixer until thoroughly blended. Add the soy milk, nondairy yogurt, and vanilla extract and beat until thoroughly blended.

Add the flour mixture in two batches, mixing each time until just combined. Don't overmix; a few little lumps are okay.

Spread the batter in the prepared pans, dividing it evenly between them. Bake for 20 to 25 minutes, until a toothpick inserted in the center comes out clean.

Let cool for about 15 minutes. Carefully turn each pan upside down on top of a wire cooling rack. Gently tap the bottoms of the pans to loosen the cakes. You may need to run a butter knife around the edges to loosen the cakes from the pans. Let cool completely before frosting.

To make the frosting, sift the confectioners' sugar and cocoa powder into a medium bowl and mix well.

Put the margarine in a large bowl or the bowl of a stand mixer fitted with the paddle attachment. Beat with a handheld mixer or the stand mixer until creamy. Add half of the sugar mixture and 2 tablespoons of the soy milk and beat until creamy. Add the remaining sugar mixture, the remaining 3 tablespoons of soy milk, and the vanilla extract and beat until fluffy.

Per serving (based on 16 servings): 360 calories, 4 g protein, 13 g fat (4 g sat), 57 g carbs, 258 mg sodium, 65 mg calcium, 1 g fiber

To assemble the cake, put 1 cake layer top-side up on a serving plate or cake stand. If the top is rounded, carefully slice it off to make a flat surface. Spread about one-quarter of the frosting evenly over the top.

Put the other cake layer on the frosting, top-side up. Spread the remaining frosting evenly over the top and sides of the cake. Refrigerate until ready to serve.

NOTE: The addition of turmeric to the cake batter may seem a bit odd. No worries; the amount is small enough that it doesn't flavor the cake, yet there's enough to give these layers that distinctive yella' cake color.

COCONUT ICEBOX CAKE: This variation for coconut-covered yella' cake tastes better and becomes more moist after a night of refrigeration—if you can wait that long. The only difference is the frosting. Instead of making the chocolate frosting, simply stir together 3 cups of unsweetened shredded dried coconut, 12 ounces of vegan sour cream, and ¾ cup of confectioners' sugar until thoroughly blended. Frost the cake as described in the main recipe and refrigerate until ready to serve.

 emphis's own Elvis Presley had a well-known penchant for fried peanut butter and banana sandwiches. I think the King would have given me a big "Thank ya, thank ya very much" for these muffin-like cupcakes flecked with bits of banana and crushed peanuts and topped with a luscious peanut butter frosting.

Peanut Butter and Banana Cupcakes with Peanut Buttercream

See photo facing page 151.

MAKES 12 CUPCAKES

CUPCAKES

1¼ cups unbleached all-purpose flour

1 teaspoon baking powder

½ teaspoon salt

¼ teaspoon baking soda

½ cup chopped peanuts

1 cup mashed ripe banana

⅔ cup plain soy milk

½ cup sugar

⅓ cup unsweetened applesauce

2 tablespoons sorghum syrup or
    blackstrap molasses

1 teaspoon vanilla extract

To make the cupcakes, preheat the oven to 350 degrees F. Line a 12-cup standard muffin tin with paper or foil liners.

Sift the flour, baking powder, salt, and baking soda into a large bowl and stir to combine. Stir in the peanuts.

Put the banana, soy milk, sugar, applesauce, sorghum syrup, and vanilla extract in a medium bowl and stir until thoroughly blended.

Make a well in the flour mixture. Pour in the banana mixture and stir until just combined. Don't overmix.

Spoon the batter into the lined muffin cups, distributing it evenly and filling each cup about three-quarters full. Bake for 22 to 25 minutes, until a toothpick inserted in the center of a cupcake comes out clean.

Let cool in the tin for 5 minutes. Transfer the cupcakes to a wire cooling rack and let cool completely before frosting.

Per cupcake: 429 calories, 9 g protein, 20 g fat (6 g sat), 56 g carbs, 160 mg sodium, 46 mg calcium, 3 g fiber

There's no oil in these cupcakes, so they're actually pretty low in fat. Think of the cake part as "skinny Elvis." However, the frosting—made with shortening, peanut butter, and plenty of sugar—is "fat Elvis" in all his rhinestoned, chubby-cheeked glory.

PEANUT BUTTERCREAM

½ cup nonhydrogenated vegetable shortening

½ cup creamy natural peanut butter

3 cups confectioners' sugar

5 tablespoons plain soy milk

1 teaspoon vanilla extract

GARNISHES

½ cup chopped peanuts

12 dried banana chips (optional)

To make the buttercream, put the shortening and peanut butter in a large bowl or the bowl of a stand mixer fitted with the paddle attachment. Beat with a handheld mixer or the stand mixer until thoroughly blended. Add the confectioners' sugar, 1 cup at a time, and beat until fluffy. Add the soy milk and vanilla extract and beat until very fluffy.

To frost and garnish the cupcakes, spread or pipe the buttercream in swirls over the tops of the cooled cupcakes (see note). Sprinkle about 2 teaspoons of the peanuts on each cupcake and top with a dried banana chip if desired.

NOTE: To make your own pastry bag, scoop the buttercream into a large ziplock bag. Push any air out of the bag, then seal it and trim off a tiny corner with scissors. Use your makeshift pastry bag to squeeze buttercream over the cupcakes in a fancy circular pattern, beginning on the outside edge of the cupcakes and working your way in.

Traditional mole sauce contains savory ingredients like chicken broth and onions, but those flavors have no place in a cupcake—especially a vegan one! The mole sauce in this recipe features a combination of ancho chile powder, sesame seeds, dark chocolate, almonds, and cinnamon, resulting in a unique sweet 'n' spicy cupcake.

Holy Mole Chocolate-Chile Cupcakes with Cinnamon Buttercream

MAKES 12 CUPCAKES

CUPCAKES

3 dried ancho chiles

3 tablespoons sesame seeds

1 cup plain soy milk

½ cup dark chocolate chips or chunks, at least 60 percent cacao

¾ cup sugar

⅓ cup canola oil

1 teaspoon vanilla extract

½ teaspoon almond extract

½ cup slivered almonds

¼ cup raisins

1 teaspoon ground cinnamon

1¼ cups unbleached all-purpose flour

¾ teaspoon baking powder

½ teaspoon baking soda

¼ teaspoon salt

To make the cupcakes, preheat the oven to 350 degrees F. Line a 12-cup standard muffin tin with paper or foil liners.

Remove the stems and seeds from the chiles and discard them. Put the chiles in a small food processor or clean coffee grinder and process until powdery. Measure out 3 tablespoons of the powdered chiles and set aside. Reserve any remaining ground chiles for garnish.

Toast the sesame seeds in a dry skillet over low heat, stirring frequently, until lightly browned and fragrant, 1 to 2 minutes.

Put the soy milk and chocolate in a small saucepan over medium heat. Stir constantly until the chocolate is melted. Remove from the heat and stir in the sugar, oil, vanilla extract, and almond extract.

Put the 3 tablespoons of powdered chiles and the sesame seeds, almonds, raisins, and cinnamon in a food processor and process until the texture resembles coarse cornmeal. Add the chocolate mixture in two additions, processing after each addition and stopping occasionally to scrape down the work bowl and move the mixture toward the blades. After the second addition, process just until the mixture is thick and chunky.

Sift the flour, baking powder, baking soda, and salt into a large bowl and mix well. Add the chocolate mixture and stir until just combined.

Spoon the batter into the lined muffin cups, distributing it evenly and filling each cup about three-quarters full. Bake for 20 to 22 minutes, until a toothpick inserted in the center of a cupcake comes out clean.

Let cool in the tin for 5 minutes. Transfer the cupcakes to a wire cooling rack and let cool completely before frosting.

Per cupcake: 464 calories, 4 g protein, 28 g fat (8 g sat), 51 g carbs, 210 mg sodium, 71 mg calcium, 2 g fiber

CINNAMON BUTTERCREAM

½ cup nonhydrogenated vegan margarine

½ cup nonhydrogenated vegetable shortening

2 cups confectioners' sugar

1 teaspoon vanilla extract

1 teaspoon ground cinnamon

To make the buttercream, put the margarine and shortening in a large bowl or the bowl of a stand mixer fitted with the paddle attachment. Beat with a handheld mixer or the stand mixer until soft and creamy. Add the confectioners' sugar, 1 cup at a time, and beat until fluffy. Add the vanilla extract and cinnamon and beat until very fluffy.

To frost and garnish the cupcakes, spread or pipe the frosting in swirls over the tops of the cooled cupcakes (see note, page 159). Sprinkle with as much of the reserved ground chiles as desired.

Imagine pumpkin pie in cupcake form, and you've got these delectable little autumn-inspired treats. The cupcakes boast the glorious flavors that celebrate the harvest: allspice, cinnamon, cloves, and nutmeg. The fluffy pumpkin buttercream is tasty enough to eat by itself with a spoon, but resist temptation and put it on the cupcakes instead.

Vanilla-Spice Cupcakes with Pumpkin Buttercream

MAKES 12 CUPCAKES

CUPCAKES

1½ cups unbleached all-purpose flour

¾ cup sugar

2 tablespoons cornstarch

1 teaspoon baking powder

1 teaspoon ground cinnamon

½ teaspoon baking soda

¼ teaspoon salt

¼ teaspoon ground allspice

¼ teaspoon ground cloves

¼ teaspoon ground nutmeg

1 cup plain soy milk

3 tablespoons unsweetened applesauce

2 tablespoons canola oil

1½ teaspoons vanilla extract

To make the cupcakes, preheat the oven to 350 degrees F. Line a 12-cup standard muffin tin with paper or foil liners.

Put the flour, sugar, cornstarch, baking powder, cinnamon, baking soda, salt, allspice, cloves, and nutmeg in a large bowl and mix well.

Put the soy milk, applesauce, oil, and vanilla extract in a medium bowl and whisk until thoroughly blended. Pour into the flour mixture and stir until just combined. Be careful not to overmix; a few little lumps are okay.

Spoon the batter into the lined muffin cups, distributing it evenly and filling each cup about three-quarters full. Bake for 20 to 22 minutes, until a toothpick inserted in the center of a cupcake comes out clean.

Let cool in the tin for 5 minutes. Transfer the cupcakes to a wire cooling rack and let cool completely before frosting.

Per cupcake: 330 calories, 2 g protein, 11 g fat (4 g sat), 56 g carbs, 137 mg sodium, 37 mg calcium, 1 g fiber

PUMPKIN BUTTERCREAM

½ cup nonhydrogenated vegetable
  shortening

⅓ cup pumpkin purée

3 cups confectioners' sugar

1 teaspoon vanilla extract

1 teaspoon ground cinnamon

Pinch ground allspice

Pinch ground cloves

Pinch ground nutmeg

1 teaspoon plain soy milk, if needed

To make the buttercream, put the shortening and pumpkin puree in a large bowl or the bowl of a stand mixer fitted with the paddle attachment. Beat with a handheld mixer or the stand mixer until smooth and creamy. Add the confectioners' sugar, 1 cup at a time, and beat until fluffy. Add the vanilla extract, cinnamon, allspice, cloves, and nutmeg and beat until very fluffy. Add the teaspoon of soy milk if the buttercream doesn't seem fluffy enough and beat for 1 minute.

To frost the cupcakes, spread or pipe the buttercream in swirls over the tops of the cooled cupcakes (see note, page 159).

T alk of the Old South conjures images of a Southern belle in a hoop skirt, wielding a fan in one hand and cradling a mint julep in the other. These cakey brownies combine bourbon and mint (the key ingredients in a mint julep) with luscious chocolate for a tasty, cocktail-inspired treat. Since they're made with applesauce rather than oil, you should still be able to squeeze into your corset after eating the whole pan.

Mint Julep Brownies

MAKES 9 TO 16 BROWNIES

½ cup crumbled firm silken tofu

¾ cup unsweetened applesauce

¾ cup sugar

2 teaspoons bourbon

1 teaspoon vanilla extract

½ teaspoon mint extract

1⅓ cups whole wheat pastry flour

¾ cup unsweetened cocoa powder

1 teaspoon baking powder

¼ teaspoon salt

1 cup semisweet chocolate chips

Preheat the oven to 350 degrees F. Spray an 8-inch square baking pan with nonstick cooking spray.

Put the tofu in a food processor and process until smooth, stopping occasionally to scrape down the work bowl and move the mixture toward the blades. Add the applesauce, sugar, bourbon, vanilla extract, and mint extract and process until smooth again, stopping occasionally to scrape down the work bowl and move the mixture toward the blades.

Sift the flour, cocoa powder, baking powder, and salt into a large bowl and mix well. Stir in the chocolate chips. Add the tofu mixture and stir until just combined. Spread the batter in the prepared pan.

Bake for 22 to 25 minutes, until the center looks set and bounces back slightly when touched. Let cool completely before cutting the brownies to the desired size.

Per brownie (based on 12 brownies): 190 calories, 4 g protein, 5 g fat (3 g sat), 33 g carbs, 77 mg sodium, 51 mg calcium, 4 g fiber

hocolate chip cookies are great. Chocolate–chocolate chip cookies are better. But throw in some candied pecans, and you've got yourself one heck of a cookie. By the way, the pecans are pretty tasty on their own, so you might want to make extras for snackin' on.

Choco–Chocolate Chip Praline Cookies

MAKES 36 TO 42 COOKIES

CANDIED PECANS

¾ cup coarsely chopped pecans

1 teaspoon canola oil

Pinch salt

2 tablespoons maple syrup

COOKIES

3 tablespoons water

1 tablespoon ground flaxseeds

1 cup nonhydrogenated vegan margarine, at room temperature

1 cup sugar

1 tablespoon blackstrap molasses

2 teaspoons vanilla extract

2¼ cups whole wheat pastry flour

½ cup unsweetened cocoa powder

1 teaspoon baking soda

¼ teaspoon salt

½ cup semisweet chocolate chips

To make the candied pecans, line a baking sheet with parchment paper. Toast the pecans in a dry skillet over medium heat, stirring frequently, until lightly browned and fragrant, about 5 minutes. Add the oil and salt and cook, stirring constantly, for 1 minute. Add the maple syrup and cook, stirring constantly, until the syrup is bubbly, about 1 minute.

Transfer to the lined baking sheet, spreading the pecans in a single layer. They shouldn't be on top of each other, but it's okay if they touch; they can be broken apart later. Put the baking sheet in the refrigerator until the pecans have hardened, 20 to 30 minutes.

To make the cookies, preheat the oven to 350 degrees F. Line two large baking sheets with parchment paper.

Combine the water and flaxseeds in a small bowl and mix well.

Put the margarine and sugar in a large bowl or the bowl of a stand mixer fitted with the paddle attachment. Beat with a hand mixer or the stand mixer until creamy. Add the molasses, vanilla extract, and flaxseed mixture and beat until thoroughly blended.

Put the flour, cocoa powder, baking soda, and salt in a large bowl and mix well. Pour in the margarine mixture and stir until a dough forms. Stir in the chocolate chips.

Break any large chunks of the candied pecans into smaller, bite-sized pieces. Stir the pecans into the dough.

Scoop the mixture onto the lined baking sheets, using about 2 tablespoons of dough per cookie and leaving about 1 inch between them.

Bake for 8 to 10 minutes, until the cookies are firm.

Let cool on the baking sheets for about 5 minutes. Transfer to wire cooling racks and let cool completely.

Per cookie (based on 39 cookies): 121 calories, 1 g protein, 7 g fat (2 g sat), 13 g carbs, 96 mg sodium, 13 mg calcium, 2 g fiber

In this recipe, peanut butter cookies are jazzed up with wholesome oats and sandwiched together with vanilla buttercream. Who could ask for anything more? The fluffy buttercream certainly beats the heck out of that mystery filling in popular packaged oatmeal cream pies. The best thing about cream pie cookies? You have permission to eat two cookies instead of one, since it takes two to make a proper sandwich. But now there's a new problem: limiting yourself to just one cream pie.

Peanut Butter Oatmeal Cream Pies

MAKES ABOUT 15 CREAM PIES

COOKIES

1¼ cups whole wheat pastry flour

½ teaspoon baking soda

½ teaspoon baking powder

¼ teaspoon salt

2 cups quick-cooking rolled oats

3 tablespoons water

1 tablespoon ground flaxseeds

1 cup brown sugar, packed

½ cup creamy natural peanut butter

¼ cup plain soy milk

2 tablespoons nonhydrogenated vegan margarine, at room temperature

BUTTERCREAM FILLING

¼ cup nonhydrogenated vegetable shortening

¼ cup nonhydrogenated vegan margarine

1¾ cups confectioners' sugar

1 tablespoon plain soy milk

1 teaspoon vanilla extract

To make the cookies, preheat the oven to 350 degrees F. Line two large baking sheets with parchment paper.

Put the flour, baking soda, baking powder, and salt in a medium bowl and mix well. Stir in the oats.

Put the water and flaxseeds in a large bowl or the bowl of a stand mixer fitted with the paddle attachment and mix well. Add the brown sugar, peanut butter, soy milk, and margarine and beat with a handheld mixer or the stand mixer until thoroughly blended. Pour into the flour mixture and stir to combine.

Scoop the mixture onto the lined baking sheets, using a rounded tablespoonful of dough per cookie and leaving about 1 inch between them. Aim to get about 30 cookies from the dough. Flatten the balls into 2-inch circles by lightly pressing each cookie with your palm.

Bake for 10 to 12 minutes, until the cookies are golden brown and firm.

Let cool on the baking sheets for about 5 minutes. Transfer to wire cooling racks and let cool completely before assembling the cream pies.

To make the filling, put the shortening and margarine in a large bowl or the bowl of a stand mixer fitted with the paddle attachment. Beat with a handheld mixer or the stand mixer until soft and creamy. Add the confectioners' sugar and beat until fluffy. Add the soy milk and vanilla extract and beat until very fluffy.

To assemble the cream pies, spread about 1 tablespoon of buttercream filling on the flat (bottom) side of 1 cookie. Top with another cookie. Repeat until all the cookies are assembled.

Per cream pie: 314 calories, 5 g protein, 13 g fat (4 g sat), 45 g carbs, 148 mg sodium, 38 mg calcium, 3 g fiber

own South, the mighty Mississippi River is often called the Big Muddy due to its muddy, brown water. You won't find any real mud in these no-bake cookies—just a yummy mixture of cocoa powder, creamy peanut butter, and wholesome oats. If you've ever lived down South, you know there are times during summer when you can't abide to turn the oven on. However, that doesn't mean you don't want a sweet treat. At times like those, these cookies are the perfect solution.

Mississippi Mud Cookies

MAKES ABOUT 30 COOKIES

2 cups sugar

½ cup plain soy milk

½ cup creamy natural peanut butter

½ cup nonhydrogenated vegan margarine

3 tablespoons unsweetened cocoa powder

1 teaspoon vanilla extract

3 cups old-fashioned rolled oats

Line two large baking sheets with waxed paper or parchment paper.

Put the sugar, soy milk, peanut butter, margarine, and cocoa powder in a large saucepan and stir. It isn't necessary to completely combine the ingredients at first; stirring will be easier as the mixture heats up. Cook over medium heat, stirring often, until the mixture comes to a boil.

As soon as the mixture reaches a full, rolling boil, set a timer for 1½ minutes. Let the mixture boil undisturbed (don't stir) until the timer goes off. Remove from the heat and stir in the vanilla extract, then stir in the oats.

Scoop the mixture onto the lined baking sheets, using about 2 tablespoons per cookie. Let cool completely. The cookies will be soft at first, but they will firm up in 1 to 2 hours (see note). To speed the process, refrigerate the cookies for about 1 hour.

NOTE: When it's extremely humid outside (as it often is during Southern summers), these cookies may not set up properly. If that happens, just eat 'em with a spoon!

Per cookie: 136 calories, 3 g protein, 5 g fat (1 g sat), 19 g carbs, 36 mg sodium, 6 mg calcium, 1 g fiber

O n a family trip to New Orleans, my mom spent much of her time gobbling up the Crescent City's confectionery jewel—pecan pralines. Every time she'd bite into one, she'd let me know how delicious it was and how much I was missing out. Most pralines aren't vegan since they contain milk and butter. But Mama promised she'd invent a vegan version as soon as we got home. She kept her word, and though I never tried the dairy-laden pralines in New Orleans, my mom swears these are just as tasty.

Mama's Chocolate Pecan Pralines

MAKES 28 TO 30 PRALINES

1¼ cups sugar

¾ cup brown sugar

¼ cup plain soy milk

½ cup chocolate chips

¼ cup nonhydrogenated vegan margarine

1 teaspoon vanilla extract

2 cups pecan halves

Line two large baking sheets with parchment paper.

Put the sugar, brown sugar, and soy milk in a large saucepan and stir until thoroughly blended. Cook over medium heat without stirring until the mixture reaches the soft ball stage on a candy thermometer (between 234 and 240 degrees F). Hold the candy thermometer inside the mixture the entire time, making sure it doesn't touch the bottom of the pan. Remove the mixture from the heat.

Add the chocolate chips, margarine, and vanilla extract and stir until the chocolate is melted. Stir in the pecans.

Scoop the mixture onto the lined baking sheets, using about 1 tablespoon per praline and spacing them about ½ inch apart. Don't use your fingers to push the hot mixture out of the tablespoon. Hot sugar can cause serious burns, so use another spoon or butter knife to push the thick mixture out of the spoon.

Let cool for at least 30 minutes, until firm. If you're in a hurry to dig in, the pralines will harden more quickly in the refrigerator.

Per praline (based on 29 pralines): 138 calories, 1 g protein, 8 g fat (1 g sat), 16 g carbs, 19 mg sodium, 12 mg calcium, 1 g fiber

Index

About the Author

BIANCA PHILLIPS has been piddlin' around her mama's and granny's kitchens since she was knee-high to a grasshopper (that's Southern speak for "really little"). She hasn't had any fancy culinary training, but she's a firm believer that great Southern chefs learn to cook from the soul. The Arkansas native and current resident of Memphis, Tennessee, has a background in journalism and works as an associate editor at the Memphis Flyer, an alternative news-weekly. Bianca blogs about her daily vegan eats on her Vegan Crunk food blog, vegancrunk.blogspot. com. She's also the mother of eight fur babies—six cats and two big ol' mutts.